What's the Deal with Reverse Mortgages?

By

SHELLEY GIORDANO, B.A., M.A.

Chair, Funding Longevity Task Force

Copyright 2015 by Shelley Giordano, NMLS #895515
ISBN-13: 978-0-9964598-7-7
ISBN-10: 0996459871

People Tested
MEDIA

This book is dedicated to my mentor
Barry H. Sacks, PhD, JD

and other members of the
Funding Longevity Task Force
Marguerita Cheng, CFP®

Thomas C.B. Davison, MA, PhD, CFP®

Wade D. Pfau, PhD, CFA

John Salter, PhD, CFP®, AIFA®

Sandra Timmermann, Ed.D.

Table of Contents

Acknowledgements

First and foremost, I would like to thank Bruce McPherson of San Diego for his excellent edits. His writing style is clear and effective; his suggestions vastly improved this book. Most importantly, his understanding of reverse mortgage lending as it relates to financial planning is extraordinary.

There are many who have helped me throughout the years. I especially am grateful for the collaborative work done by the **Home Equity Retirement Specialist** team. They have toiled collectively to overcome bias and misinformation in their own financial communities. So many individuals have helped hone our message that it is difficult to name them all. Jim Spicka of Idaho often reminds me to consider the Future Value of setting up a HECM line of credit early since it will grow in lockstep with interest rates. Perhaps there in no better technician than James Veale, who is generous with his understanding of HECM intricacies. Florian Steciuch of Indiana is also an enthusiastic student of all things affecting Boomer retirement. Launi Cooper, Mark Schumacher and Jan Jordan kindly allowed me to practice on their referral partners. I would like to thank Colleen Rideout and Steve Thomas of Colorado who have done excellent work making HECM lending accessible to the NAIFA organization. Peter Klamkin and Michael Banner keep the workday fun. Thank you to Burgess Kegan and Don Graves for the work they have done in Washington and Philadelphia. Marshall Gallop of Florida shared the original Excel program that helped me develop the Housing Wealth Optimizer calculator. Thank you to

Richard San Vicente of San Ramon for finding Barry Sacks through LinkedIn and arranging to share a glass of wine together in San Franciso. Dan Mooney at HUD answers questions promptly no matter how cockamanie they may be. James Warns, a fellow graduate of the College of William and Mary in Virginia, is my most trusted adviser and is without peer in his meticulous approach to lending.

My friends Torrey Larsen and Joseph Ferraro have been endlessly encouraging. And, finally, I thank Andrew B. Weissman who has understood from the beginning that this book's message is important.

Shelley Giordano
NMLS # 895515

Preface

You'll find information on reverse mortgage lending easy to come by. Amazon carries several accessible and informative books. In addition, mortgage lenders are only too happy to provide attractive brochures as well as testimonials on DVDs. The National Reverse Mortgage Lenders Association maintains an instructive Web site with an array of resources including an index of lenders and counselors.

The approach that this book takes is a bit different because the reverse mortgage of today is so different from the reverse mortgage of yesterday. In the past, because the reverse mortgage was burdened with onerous upfront fees, the financial services community, if it considered a reverse mortgage at all, simply dismissed it or relegated it to use as a last resort. All of that has changed.

Because reverse mortgage lending has matured, financial experts have taken note. In general, reverse mortgage upfront costs are lower, and consumer safeguards have been enhanced. Because of these changes, academicians, and practitioners have begun to look at the house as a valuable asset in addition to being a home. This book is intended to provide a more detailed, in-depth analysis of how reverse mortgage lending works. You may have decided to manage your own retirement investments, or perhaps you advise retirees on how to make sure their money lasts. Regardless of your role, you will find all the details necessary to make an informed decision on whether or not housing wealth deserves more attention in retirement income planning.

What follows is a review of how reverse mortgage lending has evolved. With the near disappearance of traditional employer provided pension plans, we Baby Boomer retirees face the daunting task of making sure that we have enough money, and more specifically, enough cash *flow* to last our retirement years. Admittedly some of what you will read in this book will be highly technical. Yet the message is always the same : the prudent use of housing wealth may be the ticket to a more secure retirement.

CHAPTER 1

Introduction

Jeanne Marie Calment is the oldest documented human who ever lived. Madame Calment lived in Arles, France from February 21, 1875 to August 4, 1997. She outlived both of her daughters and her grandson by decades. Astoundingly, she lived to celebrate her 122nd birthday.

Calment funded her longevity with the world's most successful reverse mortgage.

In 1965, at the age of 90, she entered a private agreement to sell her apartment to lawyer André-François Raffray. Raffray, then 47, agreed to pay her a monthly sum of 2,500 francs until she died, at which point he would take possession of her apartment. This transaction was a rudimentary reverse mortgage. Basically, Raffray was betting that Madame Calment would die shortly, making his monthly 2,500 franc investment a sweet deal.

What he failed to take into account was the potential for human longevity. He actually died first, in 1995 at age 77, while the formidable Madame Calment kept on living. Under the terms of this private reverse mortgage, his widow was obligated to continue the payments until Calment exited the home. The Raffray family ended up paying Calment the equivalent of than $180,000, more than double the apartment's value. This reverse mortgage worked out very well for the borrower because Madame Calment beat the longevity odds, but what about the lender? Monsieur Raffray did not make out so well.

What if the circumstances had been inverted? What if Madame Calment had died a few months after "selling" her house to Monsieur Raffray? Although we do not know if Monsieur Raffray guaranteed a minimum payout, it is possible that he would have been able to buy the house for a proverbial song.

This conundrum brings us to the crux of reverse mortgage lending. With the original reverse mortgages, both the lender and the borrower were at risk depending on whether the borrower's lifespan was either short or long. The borrower's short lifespan would favor the lender ; a long lifespan subjects the lender to potential loss, just like Monsieur Raffray. Concurrently, a short lifespan would subject the borrower's estate to potential loss if very little cash is disbursed before death. No one would want to enter a reverse mortgage transaction if the lender takes the title without regard for the amount of money actually advanced to the borrower.

So how can both the borrower and the lender be protected? Enter the United States Congress.

CHAPTER 2

Who Created Reverse Mortgages?

Some people have heard that a reverse mortgage is a scheme or a scam, perpetrated on helpless seniors. Others may consider a reverse mortgage a welfare handout. Many are surprised to learn that the 100th US Congress initiated the modern reverse mortgage with the **1987 Housing and Community Development Act**, and that it was signed by President Ronald Reagan in February, 1988.

The US Congress tasked the Federal Housing Authority (FHA) with designing a reverse mortgage that protected the elderly, but would encourage lending as well. In December of 1988, the Department of Housing and Urban Development (HUD) published a notice asking potential mortgage lenders to participate in a demonstration program that "will insure up to 2,500 reverse mortgages on the homes of elderly homeowners, enabling them to turn their equity into cash." Under the Home Equity Conversion Mortgage (HECM) Insurance Demonstration, the modern reverse mortgage was born.

In this way, the FHA solved the problem of protecting both the homeowner and the lender. It modified the existing FHA insurance program to fit reverse lending. Understanding how the FHA operates in traditional lending is a helpful comparison. Created in 1934, as part of the National Housing Act, the FHA provides mortgage insurance on loans made by FHA-approved lenders throughout the United States and its territories. The FHA insures mortgages on single family and multifamily homes including manufactured homes and hospitals. It is the largest insurer of mortgages in the world, insuring over 34 million properties since its inception. In 1965 the FHA became a part of the Department of Housing and Urban Development (HUD).

At the height of the Depression, Congress and President Franklin Roosevelt created an incentive for lenders to provide financing for certain higher risk borrowers by protecting the lenders from loss. FHA insurance premiums were assessed on these loans and provided the funds to insure against loss. In traditional FHA loans, homeowners pay upfront and monthly insurance premiums that provide lenders with protection against losses should the homeowner default. The FHA lenders bear less risk because the FHA will pay a claim to the lender in the event of a homeowner's default. To qualify for insurance protection these loans must meet specific requirements established by FHA.[1]

As we know, insurance is predicated on the participation of the many to cover the losses of the few. *In other words, the participants pool funds (via paying premiums). These funds in turn transfer risk to the insurance entity.* Ingeniously, the new reverse mortgage, the FHA-insured Home Equity Conversion Mortgage (HECM) adopted the FHA insurance concept, but tinkered with it in the following ways in order to adapt to reverse mortgage needs:

1. Insurance premiums are not paid monthly but added to loan balance

2. The homeowner /estate are released from liability should the loan exceed home value

3. If home value does not cover the loan balance, the lender is protected by FHA

---

1 These requirements are listed on the HUD website: http://portal.hud.gov/ hudportal/HUD?src=/program_offices/housing/fhahistory.

As you can see, the FHA solved the problem. The resulting HECM, which includes FHA insurance, is designed to encourage lenders to finance cash disbursals, but should circumstances not go as anticipated, the lenders cannot lose on the money they have financed. Additionally, the HECM protects the homeowner (and his estate) from loss should the homeowner live so long that his loan balance grows beyond the home value. The consumer safeguards are substantial and are becoming progressively better both for the individual borrower, *and* the tax payer. Unfortunately, these HECM consumer safeguards seem to elude the financial press, and many of the financial advisers on whom many Americans rely for accurate information.

Even with HUD's continued efforts to refine the program, over time program weaknesses emerged. Especially during the housing bubble years, the HECM was used to bail out hopeless situations. Some people took reverse mortgages but did not take seriously the requirements that they keep current on tax and insurance obligations. In other cases a number of spouses were displaced when the borrower died. And finally, some borrowers used the HECM irresponsibly by drawing down their entire initial credit limits at closing, leaving no cushion for falling home values. These were serious problems and jeopardized the program and its reputation. In response, the 113th Congress passed the **Reverse Mortgage Stabilization Act of 2013**. It was enacted in to order to protect not only the non-borrowing spouses but to restore financial health to the FHA Mutual Mortgage Insurance Fund. Over the years, the HECM program has been self-sustaining; the insurance pool was never intended to be a tax payer bail-out. When the housing bubble collapsed, however, the fund's solvency was in jeopardy. HUD responded by changing lending standards and the HECM, in particular, was altered significantly. As a result the fund's economic strength is improving.[2]

Financial assessments are now a basis for HECM loan approval. To counteract the effects of potential tax and insurance defaults,

---

2 http://www.reversereview.com/nrmla-news/nrmla-news-25.html

there are formulas to set aside equity to assure that tax and insurance costs are paid. These set asides are required for those who cannot establish willingness and capacity to meet these obligations. To bolster program safety, limits have been placed on how much equity can be drawn early in the loan. Finally, a **Non-Borrowing Spouse ("NBS")** status was created to allow the spouse to defer due and payable status provided that within ninety days from the death of the last surviving borrower, the NBS can establish legal ownership or other ongoing legal right to remain (e.g., executed lease, court order, etc.) in the property securing the HECM.

So rather than some fraudulent scheme designed to fleece seniors, the modern reverse mortgage aka the HECM, is a program put in place by the government of the United States. Admittedly the HECM was not perfect at inception. The program has evolved and HUD continues to fine tune the program to provide better consumer safety as well as improved risk management for the insurance pool. It is neither bad nor good in and of itself. Its value lies in how the borrower uses it.

CHAPTER 3

What Are the Consumer Safeguards? The 4 Nevers©

Early on in HECM history potential borrowers had a very difficult time finding information on reverse mortgages. Few banks provided the product, the internet was not accessible for many, and the television commercials advertising and describing the product had not begun.

I will always remember the first call I took from a bewildered and timid customer. Mrs. Burns was salt of the earth, had paid every bill on time for her entire life, and was absolutely mortified to be making a call to a mortgage company confessing her need for information on reverse mortgages. When we got to talking, her story was heartbreaking. Her husband had bladder cancer and although the doctors were finding ways to keep him alive, their insurance was woefully inadequate. Her bills for his medical and nutritional care had mounted to the point that she was borrowing from one credit card to pay another. Her husband, understandably, had pretty much checked out as he coped with his cancer. This left her alone and frightened. Having no other resources for information, her only choice was to call a stranger. She really did not even know what questions to ask. Although we were able to help her, and even had a credit card cutting ceremony at the closing, we wanted to find an easy way, a kind of checklist, for clients so that their unconscious fears of the Reverse Mortgage Boogie Man were both uncovered and addressed when they called.

Over time we developed the 4 NEVERS list. This simple list proved to be extremely useful in helping clients confirm what they think they knew about reverse mortgages. Even more, the list helped clients stand up to well-meaning, but misinformed, friends, ministers, children and even hair dressers, who were giving them advice on whether or not to pursue a reverse mortgage.

So here it is. If you memorize the 4 NEVERS, you can have a conversation with anyone on reverse mortgages and defend your understanding against those who opine on reverse mortgages *often without the least bit of factual knowledge.* The fact is the HECM always has provided essential safeguards for the consumer from the beginning, even before the most recent legislation. So even if it is wise to avoid using the word "never" in life, homeowner fears are allayed via an understanding the HECM 4 Nevers:[3]

1. The homeowner and his estate <u>never</u> give up the title to the home.

2. The homeowner, when leaving the house, or his estate, can <u>never</u> owe more than the home's value; conversely, when the house is sold, sale proceeds in excess of the debt amount belong to the borrower /estate.

3. Even if all the money that can be borrowed through the reverse mortgage has reached its limit, the homeowner <u>never</u> has to move, provided taxes, insurance, and home maintenance are continued.

4. Monthly repayments are <u>never</u> required or expected, although voluntary payments are accepted.

---

3 © 2000. The 4 Nevers. Shelley Giordano

HECM Never #1

Remember Madame Calment? When she entered the reverse mortgage with Monsieur Raffray, she relinquished ownership of her home. It worked out well for her, but no homeowner wants to give up control of his home. With the HECM, home ownership remains with the borrower. In other words: THE BANK DOES NOT GET THE HOUSE.

The HECM is a mortgage like any other but with deferred payment. When the homeowner leaves the house, there is a mortgage attached to the home that must be paid. The homeowner's heirs can elect to pay off the HECM (but never have to pay more than 95% of the home value) by acquiring their own financing, thereby keeping the house in the family.

Alternatively, they can elect to sell the house with any remaining profit being theirs to keep. The HECM, unlike, some "old" reverse mortgages, is not used in a way that the lender can take an equity share on appreciated value. All available equity beyond the loan balance belongs to the borrower or his estate. Additionally, if the loan is "underwater" they may grant the lender a "deed in lieu," hand over the keys and literally walk away. The lender's loss is made good by the FHA insurance pool, with no recourse to the borrower or his estate.

Remember, foreclosure can happen when taxes, insurance and home maintenance are not provided by the homeowner. Taxes, insurance, and home maintenance (including HOA fees) are the only mandatory funding obligations for the borrower.

HECM Never #2

The HECM protects the borrower and his estate. The loan documents state that "no deficiency judgment may be taken against the borrower or his estate." It is not possible for the parents to leave a reverse mortgage debt to their children.

This safeguard is possible because the HECM is a non-recourse loan. When a person applies for the HECM, the borrower is not required to verify that he can pay the loan back. It is the house alone that serves as collateral for the loan. If the estate sells the house to satisfy the HECM loan balance, any remaining equity belongs to the heirs. The lender cannot access any equity beyond the loan balance. The heirs may retire the mortgage for 95% of the home's appraised value, or the loan amount, whichever is less.

HECM Never #3

Some people think that people with reverse mortgages have given their homes to the bank, and once the bank decides it has lent enough money, it can throw the homeowners to the curb and force them to move. We have already seen that the HECM protects ownership and that the borrower never gives up the title, just like any mortgage. Yet unlike other mortgages, the HECM does not have a maturity date, or an end date.

Well, technically there is an end date, but one that should not give much worry. The HECM comes due on the 150th birthday of the youngest borrower, but even Madame Calment did not get close to that. The loan does require meeting obligations of home ownership, *just as any mortgage does*. The homeowner must maintain his property taxes, *just like any mortgage*. The homeowner must maintain property insurance to protect against fire and other hazards, *just like any mortgage*. Additionally, the borrower must not allow his home to fall to ruin, *just like any mortgage*.

So let's bring up that ugly word: FORECLOSURE. In the go-go years of easy credit and rapidly increasing home appreciation, some borrowers used a reverse mortgage like an ATM. They stripped their home equity and either could not, or would not, pay their tax and insurance obligations. Under the terms of the loan, the lender was faced with foreclosing on these cases.

Foreclosing on seniors is unpleasant under any circumstances and reporters had a heyday with it. The fact is, these technical foreclosures had nothing to do with the loan being a reverse mortgage. Tax and insurance default can result in foreclosure for mortgages, period. There is nothing special about a reverse mortgage in this regard.

HECM Never #4

However, there is something special about reverse mortgages and foreclosure beyond taxes and insurance. The risk of foreclosure with a HECM is fundamentally and drastically different. This is because monthly payments are never required. Therefore, no foreclosure based on non-payment can ever happen.

So think about this: is Homeowner #1, who carries a traditional mortgage requiring monthly debt service, better off than Homeowner #2, who cannot lose his home by missing payments? Whether or not you can answer this question, you must admit that there is greater risk of foreclosure for anyone holding a standard amortizing loan (with payments) versus a reverse mortgage (with no payments required). As long as taxes, insurance and maintenance obligations are met, the HECM persists until the last borrower, or Eligible Non-Borrowing Spouse dies, moves, or sells.

The HECM documents state this feature in unambiguous terms:

> *No Deficiency Judgments. Borrower shall have no personal liability for payment of the debt secured by this Security Instrument. Lender may enforce the debt only through sale of the Property. Lender shall not be permitted to obtain a deficiency judgment against Borrower if the Security Instrument is foreclosed. If this Security Instrument is assigned to the Secretary upon demand by the Secretary, Borrower shall not be liable for any difference between the mortgage insurance benefits paid to Lender and the outstanding indebtedness, including accrued interest, owed by Borrower at the time of the assignment.*

In other words, once the lender assigns the loan to FHA ("the Secretary" of HUD), the borrower has no personal responsibility for the loan. Regardless of what the loan balance becomes, and as long as home ownership obligations are met, the HECM is totally open-ended. The home is there to serve the borrower for as long as he or she lives in the house, all thanks to FHA insurance.

Conclusion

The FHA Home Equity Conversion Mortgage remains the gold standard in reverse mortgage lending. Over the years proprietary reverse mortgages with similar consumer safeguards have been marketed but the HECM continues to provide the highest loan to value, lowest rates, and most flexibility. But because the FHA Lending Limit is capped today at $625,500, homeowners with high mortgage balances may have to explore products not insured by FHA, known in the mortgage business as "Jumbo" reverse mortgages.

CHAPTER 4

What Are the Differences Between the HECM and Traditional Lending?

The Consumer Federal Protection Bureau found that some consumers do not understand, from watching commercials, that interest is compounding, or that proceeds are debt, not income. [4] Yet by definition, a reverse mortgage is a negatively amortizing loan. That means that the loan balance grows from month to month because interest payments are deferred. Interest not paid is added to the amount due. The following month's interest is calculated on the new, higher loan balance. Over time, the HECM loan balance can grow quickly.

Amortize literally means "kill the debt." In a traditional loan, periodic monthly payments reduce the debt over time. Payments are applied to the interest and a small amount to the principal. Over time, the principal does decline but the cumulative payments can easily be 2-3 times the original principal amount. Of course, it is the interest payment that reimburses the lender for "carrying the debt" all those years.

In a traditional mortgage, the homeowner is eligible to borrow an amount based on the home value, his credit profile, interest

4 http://www.consumerfinance.gov/blog/consumer-advisory-dont-be-misled-by-reverse-mortgage-advertising/

rates and the required down payment. The "more skin in the game" a homeowner provides in a down payment, the more favorable the loan terms may be.

In reverse mortgage lending, the credit available at the outset of the loan is generally less. A borrower must be at least 62 and have obtained a counseling certificate from an FHA-approved counselor. The property is subject to FHA lending codes and must either pass an FHA appraisal or brought to standards before or soon after closing.

Although a HECM is not required to negatively amortize, it is assumed that the loan will have a growing loan balance. A homeowner always may elect to keep the loan balance low by making voluntary payments to offset interest accrual. Usually, though, homeowners do not reduce debt because they decide against making any payments on either the interest or principal. To accommodate that growing debt, there must be a cushion of equity to pay the loan back. The HECM initial credit limit, therefore, is determined in part by age, and prevailing interest rates.

Figure 4.1

FHA Calculation for Determining How Much Equity Can Be Accessed at Loan's Inception

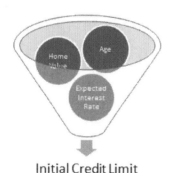

Initial Credit Limit

The initial credit limit, is known as the Initial Principal Limit. The initial credit available will grow month over month.

Because the FHA insures the loan, a HECM is subject to the FHA Lending Limit which at this printing, is $625,500. A house can be worth more the $625,000, of course, and still qualify for a reverse mortgage but values beyond the Lending Limit are invisible for purposes of calculating available credit.

The age of the youngest participant and the expected interest rate determine the Principal Limit Factor. This factor adjusts the initial maximum borrowing limit based on actuarial assumptions and what the interest rate over the course of the loan may be. HUD frequently alters the Principal Limit Factors and sometimes the Lending Limit in order to manage program risk.

Principal Limit Factors are published by the Secretary of HUD and are based on these underlying concepts, subject to the overall FHA lending limit:

- **The greater the home value** the greater amount that may be borrowed.

- **The older the borrower** the greater amount that may be borrowed.

- **The lower the interest rate** the greater amount that may be borrowed.

What if?

What if the FHA assumptions fail on any given loan? Say rising interest rates cause the loan balance to outstrip the home value? What if the client lives to 122? What if housing values drop? That's what the FHA Mortgage Insurance pool is for: protection for both the lender and the borrower. The borrower is insulated from any loss. The lender's loss in covered by FHA insurance.

How are Funds Distributed in Reverse Mortgages?

Although these features will be discussed later, it is helpful to understand that reverse mortgage draws are flexible throughout the life on the loan, particularly when the adjustable rate mortgage is chosen, provided the credit limit is not exhausted. The options for drawing on the adjustable rate HECM are:

- **Lump Sum** A draw on funds up to the current credit limit.

- **Tenure Payment** A guaranteed monthly payment as long as the last borrower lives in the house.

- **Term Payment** A monthly payment for a predetermined term.

- **Line of Credit** Credit held in reserve, but growing in capacity monthly.

- **Combination** A combination of any of the above.

Although the house does not need to be free of mortgages, whatever liens exist must be paid off either by the homeowner or through the proceeds available at the loan's outset.

How are Costs Paid?

Since actuarial tables and prevailing interest rates determine how much a homeowner may borrow at the outset of the loan, repayment can be deferred until the last borrower dies, moves, or sells. Closing costs, lender fees, and the initial FHA MIP are rolled into the loan and become part of the loan balance. As the mortgage progresses any draws, annual MIP, and loan costs are added to the loan balance. At the loan's end, either the borrower or his estate still retain ownership and will have to decide how to pay back the loan balance. This is done either by selling the house (and keeping remaining equity) or keeping the house by arranging new financing. If the house is underwater, neither the borrower nor his estate, have an obligation to make good on the loan. In this situation, the estate may retire the loan for 95% of appraised value regardless of the loan amount outstanding.

Chart 4.2

Comparison of Initial Debt versus Home Value

In the chart below, notice how a traditional mortgage would compare to a reverse mortgage. In this example, the homeowner qualifies to borrow 90% of the home's value. The upper segment represents the 10% down payment that he made on the house. The homeowner will be making payments to pay off the debt for 20-30 years. Thus the lower segment will diminish (and the upper segment will increase) during that period. On a $400,000 initial loan amount at 5% interest, this borrower would have paid **$373,000** in interest over 30 years, making the total payback $773,000.

As we have seen, the HECM credit limit is determined by the borrower's age when the loan is initiated. The older the homeowner, the more money may be borrowed. Actuarial tables predict that any given older person will generally exit the home sooner than a younger person. And since the house pays the loan back, younger people will have less initial access to funds than older ones.

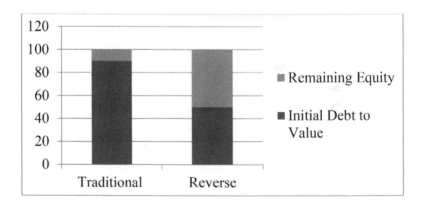

Comparison of Final Equity versus Home Value

In this example, the homeowner is in his 60's and qualifies for a reverse mortgage loan equal to 50% of the home value. Because the loan balance will be going up during the ensuing year (unless voluntary payments are made), the amount that he can borrow is limited, as he can be expected to live in the home many more years.

The upper segment here represents the cushion to accommodate the rising debt. Thus, during the period in which the borrower remains in the house, the lower segment (debt) will increase, and the upper segment (equity) will diminish.

The chart below compares a traditional mortgage with a reverse mortgage at the end of the loan. The traditional loan has been completely paid off although the homeowner has "paid out" 2-3 times the home value to the lender in interest and principal. The time value burden is significant in traditional lending when considering the loss of cash flow over many years. Via monthly payments, the money you have in your pocket today is slowly buying back your equity.[5] In contrast, the reverse debt will keep growing until the last borrower dies, moves or sells, unless the homeowner has elected to make payments. In this example, no payments were made during the loan term and therefore, the reverse debt reduced the remaining equity month after month. In fact, the borrowers lived so long that loan balance is higher than home's value. The loan is underwater.

Chart 4.3

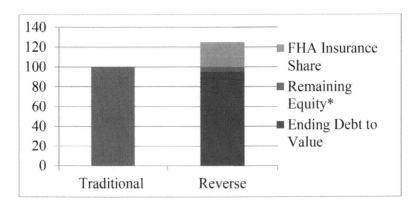

*The 5% equity that the heirs retain also is part of FHA insurance share.

---

5 *Jim Spicka. Private Correspondence.*

Again, the HECM is unique in regard to how an underwater situation is resolved:

> *"Only the HECM allows the possibility of not having to pay back all the money you might someday owe. The FHA Mortgage Insurance guarantees that no matter what you actually owe, you only have to repay what you get "NET" from the sale of the property REGARDLESS of the amount actually owing on your mortgage. This is not possible with a forward mortgage without risking default and foreclosure."*[6]

In this example, however, the borrower's heirs have decided to refinance the house and keep it in the family. The heirs are obligated to pay either the loan balance, or 95% of the home's value, whichever is less. In other words they retain 5% of the home's value, even if their parents had lived so long in the house that their loan balance exceeds the value of the house. In this underwater scenario, the lender will be made whole by the FHA. Both sides of the transaction have been protected.

REMEMBER: If the heirs decide to just go ahead and sell the house, and the loan is not underwater, they are entitled to whatever dollars the house brings beyond the actual HECM loan balance.

Chart 4.4

Comparison of HECM Loan Features versus Traditional Mortgage

	HECM Reverse	Traditional
Debt to Value (LTV) Rises	Yes	No
Monthly Payments	Voluntary	Required, can be 2-3 x original debt
Foreclosure	No for missing payments	Can result if payments not met

This chart demonstrates how a traditonal mortgage compares to a reverse mortgage.

---

6 *Jim Spicka, Private Correspondence*

Conclusion

Although many aspects of a HECM resemble those of any mortgage, the differences are significant. Often homeowners are surprised that they initially do not qualify for as large a percentage of the home value as they would in a traditional mortgage. At current interest rates, a rule of thumb for borrowers in their sixties is about 50%.

The HECM program is designed to allow the home itself to pay the loan back, not the homeowner, so there must be a cushion of equity. The remaining equity serves as a reserve to accommodate a rising loan balance but any amount of the cushion remaining at the end of the loan remains in the hands of the owner or estate.

CHAPTER 5

How About a HELOC versus a HECM Line of Credit?

Oftentimes homeowners contact their banks in order to initiate a HELOC (Home Equity Line of Credit). They want a standby emergency fund just in case they need cash quickly for unexpected expenses. Some set up this liquid fund and never even draw from the credit line. And if a HELOC borrower does not take draws, he, of course, does not make monthly repayments to the bank. Once he does draw on this credit line, monthly payments must commence.

In addition, he will need to prove to the bank that he personally can repay the HELOC loan. Some retirees are shocked to find that qualifying can be difficult because a retiree commonly has no regular income. The bank will look at the individual's income, assets, and credit score. Without income from a job, many retirees just cannot qualify for a HELOC, or for a mortgage of any kind. Ben Bernanke, former Chairman of the Federal Reserve, brought this issue into focus when he confessed that he had been turned down himself for a refinance of his mortgage.

Like the HELOC, the HECM Line of Credit can serve as a standby emergency fund. In fact, the FHA has rewarded homeowners who elect to use their equity conservatively. Significant changes were made to the program in September, 2013. Information published before that date will not reflect HUD changes.

To discourage equity-stripping, the new HECM prohibits full draws on available equity for the first year, except for defined mandatory obligations. In doing so, the FHA has established an **Initial Disbursement Level** for calculating initial insurance costs. Those who leave approximately 40% or more of their total credit amount in a line of credit until at least **Day 366** of the loan's life are charged an upfront Mortgage Insurance Premium of only .5% of the home value (but never more than the Lending Limit). In contrast the borrower who leaves less than 40% of their total initial credit limit in the line of credit before Day 366 will be charged 2.5% of home value. Of course, like a HELOC, interest is not charged against the HECM line until money is actually drawn. This, however, is where the similarity ends.

Qualifying for a HELOC in Comparison to a HECM Line of Credit

Again, to qualify, there must be one borrower at least 62 years old with a property insurable by FHA lending standards. FHA regulations have changed and beginning April, 2015 borrowers are required to demonstrate willingness and ability to meet tax, insurance, and maintenance obligations. These new underwriting requirements will not rely on credit scores or be as stringent as traditional lending. Remember, the property alone pays the loan back, not the individual. Going forward, however, the HECM will be available only to those who can demonstrate financial wherewithal to satisfy homeowner obligations for tax, insurance, and maintenance.

Set-up Costs for HECM v. HELOC

Unlike the past, a HECM Line of Credit can be established for the same cost as a HELOC. To do this, the homeowner negotiates origination fee and closing costs by selecting a particular interest rate. (The higher interest rates allow for lower origination fees and closing costs.) Some lenders today will initiate a HECM for as little as $125 if the client chooses a higher interest rate.

Protection Against Deteriorating Market Forces

People are surprised by yet another aspect of HECM lending. No matter what the economy does, no matter if housing values drop in the neighborhood, no matter what happens to the lender in the future, the HECM Line of Credit cannot be canceled, frozen, or reduced!

Many financial planners remember the fate of standby HELOCs their clients had in place for a rainy day when the Great Recession hit. Just when their clients needed ready cash, the banks canceled, reduced, or froze their lines of credit. In contrast, clients who had an FHA-insured HECM line of credit were insulated from this liquidity shock because the lender cannot alter the obligation to lend remaining funds in the HECM Line of Credit.

Chart 5.1

Comparison of HECM Line of Credit and HELOC

Loan Terms	HECM Line of Credit	HELOC
Lender can cancel, freeze or reduce line	No	Yes
Monthly payments required	No	Yes
Credit score qualifiers	No *Must demonstrate ability to meet homeowner obligations*	Yes
Deficiency judgment possible	No	Yes
Payments recast to include principal payments	No	Yes
Line of Credit in place regardless of home value	Yes	Maybe not
Unused LOC grows every month[7]	Yes	No

---

7 The HECM Line of Credit, if an adjustable rate is selected, must grow in borrowing power at a guaranteed percentage determined at closing. As long as the credit line is not exhausted, the lender is contractually obligated to make available more credit every single month at the same rate the loan balance is growing. Technically, the growth in borrowing power increases every month at the applicable monthly interest rate plus 1/12 of the yearly MIP, if there are no "set- asides" in place.

As we have learned, the credit capacity in HECM lending is known as the Principal Limit. Because the typical HECM loan balance is growing every month, negatively amortizing, the credit capacity increases every month. The available credit *not* yet drawn is termed the HECM Line of Credit. And that HECM Line of Credit increases every month in at the same rate as the Principal Limit.

The fact that the HECM Line of Credit increases every month is unique to the HECM. Borrowers and advisers alike are surprised, and even a bit bewildered, when they learn of this feature since there is no other financial product that provides a guaranteed growth like this.

5.2

Relationship of Principal Limit to Loan Balance and Line of Credit (Simplified)

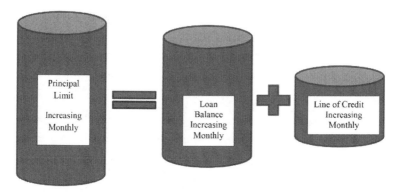

The ongoing Principal Limit is the sum of the outstanding loan balance plus a Line of Credit. The Principal Limit, the loan balance, and available Line of Credit are all increasing at the applicable interest rate and MIP. [8]

---

8 *NOTE: If the loan servicer assesses servicing fees, and/or set asides, the formula could be different. In some cases, in low interest rate environments, the line of credit actually could decrease in a given month.* **Even though the credit line may shrink in some circumstances, the overall credit capacity has not diminished. Rather, a portion of the equity is tied up in set asides.** *For a discussion of under what circumstances a LOC could shrink see* http://reversemortgagedaily.com/2009/06/02/negative-loan-growth-hits-reverse-mortgage-credit-lines/

Regardless of whether or not a client starts borrowing early, or waits to access his line of credit, he will have the same borrowing power, or credit capacity over time. In most HECM loans today, the Principal (credit) Limit minus loan balance equals Line of Credit.

Chart 5.3

Components of Principal Limit for HECM Adjustable Rate

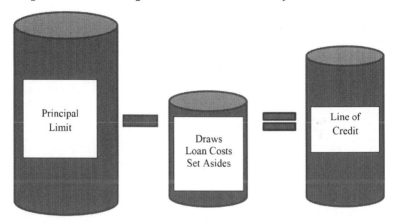

The available LOC in adjustable rate HECMs will be the difference between the Principal Limit, Draws, Loan Costs, and Set-Asides.

Chart 5.4

HECM Lump Sum Draw Versus Line of Credit Availability/Day 366

	HECM Withdrawal	Initial Loan Balance	Line of Credit
Client A	Full Draw at Closing	Closing Costs Lump Sum Draw Upfront MIP (2.5%)	$0
Client B Same Age Same Home Value Same Interest Rate Same Initial Credit	Leaves Equity in Line of Credit	Closing Costs Upfront MIP (.5%)	Growing at Applicable Monthly Interest Rate Plus 1/12 Ongoing Yearly MIP (1.25%)

Client A elects to take a full draw at closing (subject to eligibility). His Upfront Mortgage Insurance Premium (MIP) is 2.5% of home value (up to $625,500). His loan balance will be growing at the monthly applicable interest rate plus 1/12 the MIP. He will not have money left for future draws on a Line of Credit. Client B, of exactly the same age and home value and interest rate, elects to leave his equity in a line of credit. He will have access to the same overall credit because his line is growing at the same rate as Client A's loan balance. Client A's equity would have been reduced 2.5% for MIP insurance, whereas Client B's MIP load would be .5%. The client who does not take a draw at the beginning is not penalized as his credit opportunity grows with the increasing Line of Credit.

Conclusion

Many advisers and retirees recognize the wisdom of establishing an emergency fund to meet possible needs down the road in retirement. In the past a HECM could not compete with a HELOC because the set up fees were so high. Today, however, a retiree would do well to compare a HECM to a HELOC before deciding which standby fund makes the most sense. The set-up costs are now comparable, as we have seen, but the stability and flexibility provided by the HECM is worth evaluating in making the choice. Furthermore, the guaranteed growth in the HECM Line of Credit is both unique and powerful for the homeowner making decisions today on what the future value of his home could be as a means of supplementing income in retirement.

CHAPTER 6

What Are the Repayment Options in Reverse Mortgage Lending?

We have seen how a HECM Line of Credit compares to a bank HELOC. Because no payments are ever required or expected, but are accepted, the borrower can choose from an array of payment methods:

- Paying loan balance in full is known as prepayment. There is no prepayment penalty with a HECM.

- Making payments on the interest and/ or MIP, and none on the principal.

- Making voluntary payments anytime it is convenient.

- Borrower/ Heir makes a balloon payment when the last one dies, moves, or sells. Using the home itself to pay back the loan and having no responsibility for any sums underwater.

Feature One: A prepayment penalty can never be assessed against a homeowner who decides to change his mind about his reverse mortgage. If, for example, a couple initiates a reverse mortgage and then wins the lottery the next month, the loan balance may be paid in full and extinguished without penalty. Scenarios like this happen, for example, when borrowers decide to move closer to the children. The title remains with the borrower; he maintains full control over the property and there is no extra cost in "paying off" earlier than expected.

Note that a prepayment amount in excess of the outstanding balance is not allowed.

Feature Two: Payments may be made against the loan balance in any amount selected by the homeowner. This feature has solved a problem for the thousands of people who borrowed via "Interest Only (I-O)" loans during the housing bubble. These loans usually allowed a term of ten years during which a payment against the principal was not required. In fact, from 2004-2006 a total in the order of $258 billion dollars' worth of I-O mortgages were written.

Most people understood that when the 10 year period was up, they would be facing an increased monthly payment, as the loan would be "recast" in order to start chipping away at the principal. What a lot of people did not realize was that the remaining principal amortization would be compressed. All of the principal had to be paid back in a shorter period of time, hence people saw their monthly payments double or even triple. Quite a payment shock!

Replacing a recasting I-O loan with a HECM may provide payment relief, but what if the homeowners are still working and are comfortable making a payment, just not the huge catch-up that the recast requires? The HECM provides the flexibility to do just that. Voluntary payments are allowed but never expected or required.

For example, a couple was still working when they received a reset letter from their mortgage lender. They had been making monthly payments of $959 a month on their I-O mortgage. Now the bank provided notice that their loan would recast to a fully amortizing loan. Their monthly payment would roughly double. This new payment would be a burden for them, but they were comfortable with continuing to make the same monthly payment as they were making in the I-O phase of the loan. They could solve the problem with a HECM. It is possible for them to continue making the $959 payment, just like they did on their I-O loan before it reset. The following charts illustrate the effect of this strategy and can be duplicated at the Web site www.financinglongevity.com.

Chart 6.1

First Four Months: Replacing a $200,000 Loan with a HECM and Making Voluntary Payments of $959 / month

		ASSUMPTIONS								
Borrower			Initial Home Value	$625,500.00	Mandatory Payoffs	$200,000.00	Init./Exp. Rate	3.178 % / 5.030 %		
Age of Youngest Client	65		Expected Appreciation	4.00 %	Upfront MIP Rate	2.500 %	Growth Rate	4.428 %		
Tenure Payments Begin	Year 15		Monthly Paydown	$959.00	Closing Costs & Upfront MIP	$20,637.50	Monthly MIP Rate @	0.104 %		

Modify Scenario   Print Scenario

	Managed Line of Credit		Deferred Tenure Payments		Loan Balance & Schedule				
YEAR	MONTH	LINE OF CREDIT	TENURE PAYMENT	INTEREST	MIP AMOUNT	REPAYMENT	LOAN BALANCE	HOME VALUE	HOME EQUITY
0	0	$122,762.00	$0.00	$0.00	$15,637.50	$0.00	$220,637.50	$625,500.00	$404,862.50
1		$140,054.84	$0.00	$6,986.23	$2,747.89	$11,508.00	$218,863.61	$650,520.00	$431,656.39
	1	$124,173.99	$0.00	$694.32	$229.93	$959.00	$220,492.85	$627,585.00	$407,092.35
	2	$126,591.19	$0.00	$683.94	$229.68	$959.00	$220,347.27	$629,670.00	$409,322.73
	3	$127,013.63	$0.00	$683.55	$229.53	$959.00	$220,201.35	$631,756.00	$411,553.65
	4	$128,441.31	$0.00	$683.17	$229.38	$959.00	$220,054.99	$633,840.00	$413,785.11

www.financinglongevity.com
This chart demonstrates how the HECM performs the first four months with voluntary payments of $959 a month ($11,508 yearly). Note that the loan balance is reduced each month by the difference between the amount paid ($959) and the combined Mortgage Insurance (MIP) and interest accrual. Meanwhile, in the Line of Credit column, the available credit increases substantially due to its inherent growth factor, plus the fact that reductions in the loan balance result in dollar for dollar increases in available credit.

The large 2.5% upfront MIP is necessary whenever the client draws at outset more than 60% of his Initial Principal Limit. In this case, the large draw is used to pay off the original $200,000 mortgage.

Chart 6.2

HECM Performance Years 6-20 with Voluntary Payments ($11, 508) Stopping in Year 15 Converting to Optional Tenure Draws ($39,408.13 a year)

YEAR	MONTH	LINE OF CREDIT	TENURE PAYMENT	INTEREST	MIP AMOUNT	REPAYMENT	LOAN BALANCE	HOME VALUE	HOME EQUITY
6		$298,966.24	$0.00	$6,871.37	$2,624.04	$11,508.00	$208,716.82	$791,457.05	$582,740.23
7		$281,900.53	$0.00	$6,599.80	$2,596.82	$11,508.00	$208,404.24	$823,115.33	$616,711.09
8		$285,071.65	$0.00	$6,524.80	$2,566.32	$11,508.00	$203,997.15	$856,039.94	$652,052.79
9		$309,698.33	$0.00	$6,448.21	$2,539.46	$11,508.00	$201,400.94	$890,281.54	$688,920.70
10		$335,427.99	$0.00	$6,364.27	$2,503.25	$11,508.00	$198,820.37	$925,892.80	$727,072.43
11		$362,348.82	$0.00	$6,278.63	$2,499.57	$11,508.00	$196,060.57	$962,928.51	$766,867.94
12		$390,459.38	$0.00	$6,189.12	$2,494.36	$11,508.00	$193,176.06	$1,001,445.65	$808,269.59
13		$419,848.82	$0.00	$6,095.57	$2,397.57	$11,508.00	$190,151.20	$1,041,503.48	$851,342.28
14		$450,568.95	$0.00	$5,997.79	$2,359.11	$11,508.00	$187,010.09	$1,083,163.62	$896,153.53
15		$0.00	$39,408.13	$5,752.94	$2,656.13	$0.00	$235,827.28	$1,126,490.16	$890,662.88
16		$0.00	$39,408.13	$6,335.22	$3,276.88	$0.00	$286,850.51	$1,171,549.77	$884,699.26
17		$0.00	$39,408.13	$6,691.06	$3,929.77	$0.00	$340,179.46	$1,218,411.76	$878,232.30
18		$0.00	$39,408.13	$11,720.67	$4,610.08	$0.00	$395,918.34	$1,267,148.23	$871,229.89
19		$0.00	$39,408.13	$12,528.45	$5,321.13	$0.00	$454,176.05	$1,317,834.16	$863,658.11
20		$0.00	$39,408.13	$15,417.62	$6,064.32	$0.00	$515,066.42	$1,370,547.53	$855,481.11
21		$0.00	$39,408.13	$17,392.78	$6,841.09	$0.00	$579,706.41	$1,425,969.43	$846,861.02
22		$0.00	$39,408.13	$19,466.88	$7,662.96	$0.00	$646,226.37	$1,482,384.20	$837,157.84
23		$0.00	$39,408.13	$21,614.26	$8,501.82	$0.00	$714,750.26	$1,541,679.57	$826,929.31

Variable interest rate 3.3.785 % | 4.422 % APR (HECM Line of Credit) | 13.1790 % Maximum interest rate over the life of the loan | Estimated fees, including the up-front FHA mortgage insurance premium, are $20,437.53   Advanced Options

www.financinglongevity.com

In this case the couple may decide to stop *making* payments at year 15 and start *taking* payments instead. They can elect to convert their available Line of Credit to Tenure payments. They are eligible for $39,408 per year because their line of credit had grown to over $450,000.

Chart 6.3

HECM Line of Credit Growth at Interest Rate of 3.178% with $959/mo. Balance Curtailment Through Year 15

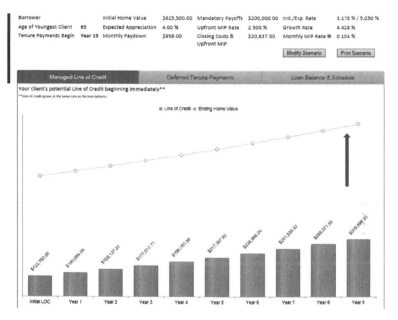

This chart displays how the Line of Credit is growing at a rate of 3.178% plus the MIP of 1.25%(4.428.) The HECM interest rate is variable and may change from month to month. If the monthly interest rate increases, the growth factor for the LOC grows in lockstep. Higher interest rates will amplify borrowing power in later years and can lower set up fees. Although the thin line demonstrates a rising home value, it is important to note that the Line of Credit grows regardless of whether or not the home value has risen or fallen, or is even underwater.
www.financinglongevity.com

Chart 6.4

Optional Conversion to Tenure Payments at Year 15

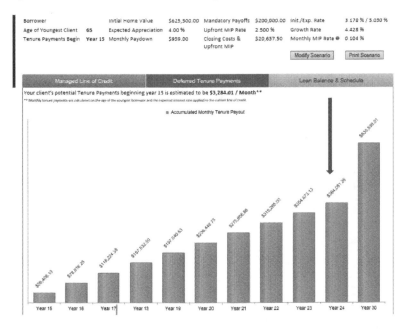

This chart displays the cumulative tenure, "annuitized" payments from Year 15-Year 30 at $3,284.01 a month ($39,408.13 a year). The total of monthly payments back to household at year 24 is $394,081.26. www.financinglongevity.com

Feature Three: Skipping payments is allowed with no repercussions. In our case study, the borrower could choose to continue making payments of $959 a month. In this example they elected to stop at Year 15. That is their right to do so. Likewise, they could have suspended payments at their discretion at any time. Perhaps they had to cope with a health shock, or needed a new roof and had to hold on to their $959. The HECM allows this without penalty since no monthly payments on the loan balance are ever expected.

Feature Four: Making a final payment at the end in one balloon payment. The HECM permits one balloon payment with no interim payments required. Technically, the balloon is not due until the last participating homeowner dies, moves, or sells.

Feature Five: Allowing a portion, or all of the house to repay the loan. When the last borrower exits the house, he or his estate will choose whether to sell the house and pay back the mortgage *or* through other means such as arranging traditional financing to pay off the HECM and retain the home. Should the loan balance be greater than the home value, the home alone will satisfy the debt. If the loan amount is less than what the house brings at sale, the borrower or his estate are entitled to remaining equity.

Conclusion: Choosing a Mortgage Plan to Meet Retirement Needs

As discussed, the HECM's flexible lending terms allow the borrower literally to custom design his own mortgage:

- Option 1: Treat it as a classic reverse mortgage to be paid back in one balloon payment

- Option 2: Use as I-O loan but without the threat of a future recast requiring principal reduction

- Option 3: Repay all draws and fees, except a $50 minimum balance, in order to keep the balance low but the Line of Credit growing

- Option 4: Start with one option but convert to another as needs in retirement change

CHAPTER 7

What Happens at Loan's End?

If the borrower(s) die or permanently move from the house, what most borrowers or heirs want to know is how long they have either to arrange new financing or sell the house to satisfy the loan balance. Not surprisingly, some fear they will be pushed into a "fire sale" situation. Yet the process for satisfying the loan is orderly as long as the borrower or heirs *stay in communication with the servicer.*

Mrs. Owens was an extremely vital and erudite 84 year old when she called about establishing a reverse mortgage. She wanted to extract money from her house to give her son a down payment for his first house. She was so cute that we filmed her for a commercial long after the closing and in doing so she showed us pictures of her swimming with her grandchildren at her son's new house. She was joyful at having shared her wealth with her family while still alive.

A couple of years later, her son Floyd called us to let us know she had died. Floyd was preparing to put mom's house on the market, and wanted the specifics on handling the reverse mortgage debt. This is where it gets tricky as debtor's remorse can overshadow the utility the mortgage provided. But in this case, Floyd was so grateful for what the reverse mortgage had enabled for both his family and his mother, that he actually thanked us for "giving" them a reverse mortgage. We were able to help him find a good Realtor© and all went smoothly.

Some folks are afraid that they will be tied to their homes and that travelling will trigger a due and payable status. Happily, HECM homeowners are not chained to their mortgaged homes. Actually "Snowbirds" are allowed to leave the home periodically as long as they maintain the property as a principal residence. Mortgagors are permitted to own multiple homes.

Some are concerned about what happens if one of the borrowers moves to a long-term care facility. This generally means that as long as one of the eligible borrowers, or Eligible Non-Borrowing Spouse (a new applicant category, see below), remains in the home, a move to a nursing home by the other is irrelevant. If there is just one remaining participant who enters a long-term care facility, the HECM remains in effect for a full year. If the last participant does not return to the home within the year, he is presumed to have moved, thus triggering a due and payable status.

Upon death, or permanent departure, of the last remaining participant, the process is as follows:

If the heirs want to keep the house in the family:

Family Pays off HECM Mortgage

Just like any other mortgage, the heirs may pay off the reverse mortgage with either cash or by acquiring their own financing. With the HECM, however, they will pay either the current loan balance or 95% of the appraised value, whichever is less.

If the borrower/heirs do not want the house and it is not underwater:

Sell Property

The borrower/heirs can sell the property and have up to a year to do so. This interval includes time extensions based on the assumption that the owner/ estate is actively working to sell the property or satisfy the debt. They must keep the loan servicer informed and prove the property is listed. Any property sales proceeds in excess of the loan balance belong to the owner/ estate. The lender is not entitled to an equity share beyond the ending loan balance. It is in the owner/estate's best interest, however, to complete arrangements quickly, because interest on the loan, as well as MIP charges, continues to accrue.

The reverse mortgage servicer provides a written payoff statement, and at closing, the loan balance is paid off, just as would be the case with any other mortgage. Again, after the loan is paid off, any and all remaining equity goes to the seller, which typically is the borrower's heirs or estate.

If the heirs want the house and it is underwater:

Short Sale

Negotiating is not permitted. The heirs may retire the loan by paying either the current loan balance or 95% of the appraised value, whichever is less.

If the heirs do not want the house and it is underwater:

Deed-in-Lieu

To avoid foreclosure, the estate can execute a Deed-in-Lieu of Foreclosure, which is a voluntary action to deed the collateral property to the servicer in exchange for a release from all obligations under the mortgage.

HECM loans are non-recourse, and the borrower and his estate CANNOT be held responsible for any shortfall. The house repays what it can, and any shortfall is covered by the FHA insurance fund.

Foreclosure

If the estate does not actively try to either sell the property, execute a short sale, or volunteer for a DIL, then there is no choice but to recoup the investment through foreclosure proceedings. Foreclosure must be approved by HUD.

The estate is entitled to the copies of the loan history, the name of the current investor, a copy of the loan documents including the mortgage note, deed of trust, and mortgage assignment, which demonstrate the right to foreclose on their loan if no other actions are taken. After a loan is due and payable, the estate benefits by communicating with the servicer to discuss and understand options to avoid foreclosure.

Eligible Non-Borrowing Spouse Deferral Period

In 2014, FHA gave new status to spouses who are not 62. In the past a spouse younger than 62 could not participate in the loan. When the loan became due, usually at the death of the older spouse, the remaining spouse would either have to move out, or attempt to refinance the HECM with her own HECM. This was not possible in many cases, especially when a full draw had been advanced, and/or property values had dropped. Worse, some unscrupulous lenders encouraged couples to drop the younger borrower so they could use the age of the older borrower to create a higher loan balance. (Remember, the older the borrower, the more initial credit is available.)

Younger spouses were forced out of their homes at the death of the older one. Greater consumer safeguards were needed to protect the younger spouse from displacement. In response to this problem, HUD/FHA created the Non-Borrowing Spouse which is defined as "…as the spouse, as determined by the law of the state in which the spouse and mortgagor reside or the state of celebration, of the HECM mortgagor at the time of closing and who also is not a mortgagor."[9]

This new category allows for a Deferral Period of the due and payable status during which the remaining spouse may continue to occupy the house. Caution: At this writing, the Deferral period is available only on the death of mortgagor (borrower) and does not apply if the mortgagor exits the home for another reason. Interest and MIP, and servicing fees (if applicable), will continue to accrue against the loan balance.

To achieve NBS status, the spouse must:

1. Have been the spouse of a HECM borrower at the time of loan closing and have *remained* the spouse of the HECM lender for the duration of the HECM borrower's lifetime;

---

9 http://portal.hud.gov/hudportal/documents/huddoc?id=14-07ml.pdf

2. Have been properly disclosed to the lender at origination and specifically named as Non-Borrowing Spouse in the HECM documents; and

3. Have occupied, and continue to occupy, the property securing the HECM as the Principal Residence of the Non-Borrowing Spouse.

Finally, the Deferral Period is allowed as long the NBS is able to establish a legal right to remain in the house.

HUD/FHA accompanied this change with a new table of credit availability (Principal Limit) factors. As always, the factor used is based on the youngest participant. These new factors allow for credit determinants as young as 18 years old. The initial credit limit, of course, is reduced accordingly due to a longer expected lifespan.

In a January 2015 Mortgagee Letter (ML 2015-02), FHA further defined the Eligible Non-Borrowing Spouse as one who can establish a legal right to remain in the home after the death, or permanent exit, of the principal borrower. This status is different from that of an "Ineligible Non-Borrowing Spouse." Those ineligible for the deferral period are deemed so because they are not legally married to the mortgagor, or do not reside in the subject property, or do not plan to reside in the subject property. When an Ineligible NBS is identified, the Principal Limit will be based on the age of the youngest HECM borrower or Eligible Non-Borrowing Spouse living in the property.

In June of 2015, HUD responded to law suits regarding former non-borrowing spouses by allowing greater latitude for lenders to assign these loans to HUD.[10] Interpretations of new regulations by lenders often result in more clarification from FHA/HUD. Readers should refer to the most recent Mortgagee Letters regarding Eligible/Ineligible Non-Borrowing Spouse status.

---

10 http://portal.hud.gov/hudportal/documents/huddoc?id=15-15ml.pdf

Caution: The Borrower Who Wants To Pay Off HECM but Continue Living In House

A borrower who wants to continue living in the house cannot take advantage of an underwater situation by paying off the mortgage using the 95% rule. In choosing to live in the house, the borrower who volunteers to extinguish the HECM would be charged the current loan balance regardless of home value. However, he would not be subject to a prepayment penalty. Once he leaves, he does maintain the right to present the lender with a deed-in-lieu. Again, once he leaves the house permanently he has no personal liability for repayment.

Summary

HUD/FHA places time constraints on the lender, as there is no economic benefit to retaining an unoccupied home. The loan is predicated on actuarial tables, so heirs cannot just move into the house and let the balance continue to accrue. Arrangements for loan disposition must be made in a reasonable time period.

"The clock starts ticking the day the last surviving borrower no longer occupies the property as a primary residence. Once the home is unoccupied, the borrower or his estate have six months to pay off the loan. In addition to the initial six months, up to two three-month extensions can be requested (for a total of one year) if more time is needed.

Extensions are not automatic; documentation that the home is listed for sale, a sale is pending, or that a family member is applying for financing on the home, is required for an extension to be granted.

The loan servicer should be contacted immediately once the home is vacant. Reverse mortgage servicers deal with these situations every day and will work with borrowers and family members. However, they can't help if they don't hear from anyone. All reverse mortgage servicers send monthly loan statements to borrowers. Those statements contain all loan and contact information necessary to make contact with the lender."[11]

---

11 *Laurie MacNaughton and Neil Sweren, "How the Back-End of a Reverse Mortgage Works," www.MiddleburgReverseLady.com, 2014*

CHAPTER 8

How Do I Use Reverse Mortgage Financing in a Home Purchase?

Advisers, Realtors©, builders and consumers are often very much surprised to learn that a HECM can be used to buy a new residence. For a period of time, Fannie Mae provided a reverse mortgage, named the Home Keeper,® that provided financing at the closing table for home purchase. Yet until the **Housing and Economic Recovery Act** of 2009, the FHA HECM could only be employed by borrowers already residing in their homes. This caused the borrower who wanted to move to a new house, and place a reverse mortgage on it, to endure two closings. The process required two steps:

1. Take title to the home (Purchase transaction)

2. Acquire the reverse mortgage (Refinance transaction)

If the borrower did not have the cash to buy the house outright in the first closing, he bore the expense of obtaining, and qualifying for, a conventional mortgage in order to complete the purchase. At some point in the future he would incur a second set of closing costs when he initiated a reverse mortgage to replace the temporary mortgage.

FHA rectified this inequity by allowing HECM funds to be disbursed at the purchase closing, thus eradicating the need for a second transaction.

Difference Between Purchasing a New Principal Residence and Buying a Second Home

HECM financing is tied to the homeowner's principal residence. Since there are no limitations on how reverse mortgage funds may be used, it always has been permissible to extract money from the permanent residence to buy a second home. This is common in families where the parents want to continue living in their legacy home but the children prefer to retain the vacation home.

Example 8.1
Buying a Second Home

Legacy home appraisal, principal residence of parents, free and clear	$500,000
Lump sum HECM eligibility (@Day 366)	$280,000
Beach House purchase price	$280,000
Mortgage on Beach House	$0

The parents use $280,000 in cash from their legacy home to purchase the family beach house.

No monthly payments are due on the beach house or the legacy home although interest and MIP will accrue on the HECM loan balance. The heirs will inherit both houses, sell the legacy home, but retain the vacation spot for future generations.

Compare the above scenario to a purchase of a new principal residence using the HECM:

Example 8.2
Buying a New Principal Residence

Cost of new home	$400,000
Lump sum HECM eligibility (@ closing)	$210,000
Down payment required	$190,000
Monthly Mortgage Payment	$0

The homeowner purchases the new home by providing a portion of the sale price as cash. The amount required is based on age and current interest rates. This cash down payment becomes "equity." Generally this cash comes from the sale of the departure home but other funds may be used. The remaining purchase funds come in the form of a lump sum reverse mortgage. The homeowners may live in the new house free of payment until the last one dies, moves, or sells.

How HECM Purchase Money is Calculated

It is difficult to envision how the HECM Purchase transaction unfolds unless you understand that the reverse mortgage financing attaches to the home being purchased, not to the home being left behind.

Illustration 8.1 Departure House Not Part of Transaction

The departure home is not used to calculate purchase money funds.

Legacy Home

HECM Reverse Mortgage is placed on new home.

This house is used to determine HECM purchase funds. The reverse mortgage attaches to the new principal residence.

New Retirement Home

Illustration 8.2

Formula for Determining Down Payment Needed to Purchase/ Examples

(Purchase Price) minus (HECM Lump Sum)* equals Down Payment

A.	$300,000	$180,000	$120,000
B.	$1,000,000	$340,000	$660,000
C.	$700,000	$300,000	$400,000

* The HECM Lump Sum draw is calculated using the HECM formula taking into account the age of the youngest borrower or Eligible Non-Borrowing Spouse, the current "Expected" interest rate and the FHA appraised value of the home or $625,500, whichever is less. Some buyers have reported that they used IRA funds to make the initial down payment. They repaid the IRA money within 60 days by selling the former home, and avoided a tax bill.

Example A. "Double Buying Power"

In this case, a widow, Mrs. Bridges, needed to move to a home nearer her children several states away. A Realtor advised her that her current home would net, after expenses, $150,000. She did not want to mortgage her new home, and even if she applied for a traditional mortgage, likely would not qualify. She had given up trying to move because the houses near her children cost $250,000 to $300,000. Her $150,000 budget would not be enough to purchase any of those houses.

Her son's financial adviser provided the solution. He advised the family to go ahead and search for a comfortable house in a good neighborhood nearby. They found a suitable home, all on one level, five minutes from the grandchildren. The house cost $300,000. Mrs. Bridges was able to purchase this house because, at her age, she qualified for a lump sum payment, from a reverse mortgage, of $180,000. Her down payment was just $120,000. This allowed her to save the unspent $30,000 from the sale of her departure home. She moved into the new house and never made a payment on interest or principal.

Example B. Buy More House

In this case, the Herberts were drawn to a luxury development in Naples, Florida. They had netted $660,000 from the sale of their legacy home in New Jersey. They were comfortable in spending this amount but did not want to dip into savings, nor take on a mortgage. When they met with the builder, however, they quickly learned that luxury options like a pool, a waterfront lot, a chef's kitchen, spa bathrooms, and other upgrades shot the potential price up to a million dollars. The builder knew of the HECM Purchase program and was able to calculate that they would qualify for a $340,000 Lump Sum payment. By combining the HECM Purchase money with the $660,000 they already had, the Herberts were able to order all the upgrades they desired. And like Mrs. Bridges, the Herberts never made a payment on interest or principal.

Example C. Conserve Nest-Egg

A financial adviser in Sacramento helped Mr. Chen manage a move to San Francisco to be with his family after his wife died. Mr. Chen sold his house in Sacramento and netted $460,000. He was faced with having to spend $700,000 for his new house in the city. Having lived through his wife's protracted illness, he was sensitive to holding on to as much cash as possible. He could manage the $700,000 purchase but would have to divest $240,000 of his brokerage account to make up the difference. And for Mr. Chen, a traditional mortgage was out the question.

Both he and his adviser were reluctant to take so much cash out of his nest egg. The adviser calculated that a HECM Purchase Lump Sum of $300,000 could be used toward the purchase. Mr. Chen's down payment, then, was $400,000. So instead of using all $460,000 of his proceeds, he "saved" $60,000 plus the $240,000 that he did not withdraw from savings:

Purchase without HECM	$700,000 Purchase Price
Net Proceeds from Departure House	**$460,000**
Portfolio Withdrawal	($240,000)
Purchase using HECM Purchase Money	**$700,000 Purchase Price**
Net Proceeds from Departure House	$460,000
HECM Purchase Money Lump Sum	$300,000
Cash Down Payment from Net Sale Proceeds	**$400,000**
Cash Retained	$240,000 + $60,000 = + $300,000

Until Mr. Chen leaves the house permanently, he will not make a payment on either the interest or the principal.

The adviser prepared a new financial plan for Mr. Chen taking into account the positive $300,000 swing in his financial profile. He demonstrated with financial software that Mr. Chen's cash flow survival probabilities were improved dramatically even though he was making this expensive move.

Summary

The HECM for Purchase program may benefit a homeowner by:

1. Eliminating monthly interest and principal payments, thus improving cash flow

2. "Doubling" the purchasing power for some homes, subject to age and interest rates

3. Enabling an upgrade to a more expensive property

4. Conserving the nest egg

Purchasers may avoid the high "2.5% MIP" typically seen in HECM for Purchase transactions by providing a high enough down payment to keep their Initial Disbursement Level at the 60% mark.

CHAPTER 9

What's the Impact of Using Housing Wealth in Retirement?

Now we going to start looking at numbers. But before going further, let's consider how difficult retirement income planning is. In fact, it is so hard the William F. Sharpe, who won the 1990 Nobel prize in Economics, called retirement-income planning the most complex problem he'd analyzed in his career.[12] Many others recognize how difficult it is to prepare for a secure retirement. Moshe Milevsky, PhD and Alexandra McQueen, CFP, for example, discuss how risky retirement is :

> *"Our quantitative analysis indicates that a prospective retiree—who could be you—might have 20, 30, or even 40 times their annual income needs in investable wealth. These assets could be sitting in the most diversified of mutual funds, investments, retirement savings accounts, or even in a DC pension plan, and yet the retiree still runs the risk that the portfolio will not last as long as he or she does. This is the nature of random and unpredictable human longevity combined with financial volatility. In the language of retirement income planning, retirement income streams without guarantees are subject to 'lifetime*

12 http://www.advisorperspectives.com/newsletters14/Bill_Sharpe_on_
Retirement_Planning.php

ruin probability'-which happens when you are alive, but your portfolio is dead."[13]

Certainly this book can make no contribution to understanding how to prevent portfolio ruin in retirement. Nevertheless we can review what the Eggheads, as we affectionately call them, are thinking about the role housing wealth *could* play in retirement.

It all started in 2004 when former physicist turned tax and pension lawyer, Barry H. Sacks, from San Francisco, started looking for a way to buffer portfolio volatility in retirement. He was aware of the risks that retirees would face once they moved out of the accumulation phase and started relying on their nest eggs for income. This concern was driven, in part, by inexorable economic realities that could jeopardize retirement for Baby Boomers:

1. Longevity Risk

Documentation abounds for how long the Boomer generation can expect to live. Wade D. Pfau, PhD, CFA, Professor of Retirement Income, The American College, notes in his blog:

> *"For a 50-year old couple, there is a 50% chance that at least one member of the couple will live at least for just under another 42 years to age 92. By the time they reach 75, there is a 50% chance that at least one will live for a little more than 17 more years to age 92. This is the age range where mortality starts to pick up. If both are still alive at age 92, there is a 50% chance that at least one will live for at least 4.6 more years to 96.6, and so on."*
> *http://retirementresearcher.com*

---

13 Milevsky, Moshe, PhD and MacQueen, Alexandra, CFP, P*ensionize Your Nest Egg.*

Chart 9.1

Longevity Risk for Opposite Sex Couples at Age 65

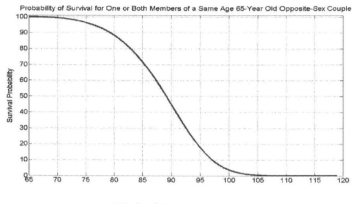

Probability of Survival for One or Both Members of a Same Age 65-Year Old Opposite-Sex Couple

Wpfau.blogspot.com

2. Risk for Funding Retirement Has Shifted to the Individual

Traditional pensions are disappearing as a vehicle to fund retirement in America. Beginning with a change to the IRS Code in 1978, the adoption of qualified plans such as the 401(k) have shifted the responsibility of funding retirement away from the employer and onto the shoulders of the individual.

With defined benefit plans, the employer provides a fixed and guaranteed payment to the retired employees. Yet the cost of funding these guarantees is variable and depends on investment returns. A defined contribution plan, in contrast, "specifies the amount the employer will contribute to a retirement account on behalf of each employee every year, and how much an employee receives in retirement will depend on"[14] what his personal account ultimately is able to provide. The cost for the employer is now fixed, but the benefit to the employee is variable, and subject to market returns.

What this means is that the individual retiree, not the employer, has to figure how to make the nest egg last!

---

14 Neuwirth, Peter, FSA. *What's Your Future Worth: Using Present Value to Make Better Decisions*

Chart 9.2
Defined Benefit Plans versus Defined Contribution Plans

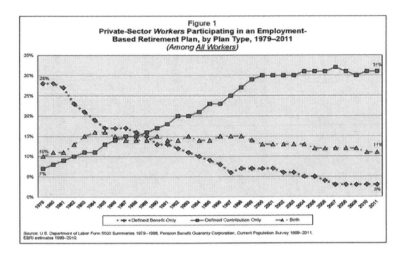

Not many Americans can count on a fixed-formula pension arrangement (Defined Benefit Plan) from their employers. Instead, the average American supposedly has provided for his own retirement by saving earnings over the years in a Defined Contribution Plan.

Not surprisingly, Americans are nervous about whether or not they have saved enough to last a long retirement. AARP reported in 2010 that the fear of running out of money exceeds the fear of death.

Chart 9.3

AARP Report on Allianz Poll: Fear of Running Out of Money

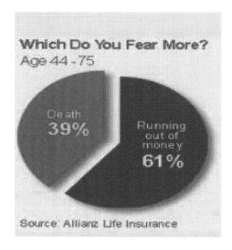

http://www.aarp.org/work/retirement-planning/info-06-2010/running_out_of_money_worse_than_death.html[15]

3. Market Volatility: Sequence of Returns Risk and Reverse Dollar Cost Averaging

Although planners disagree on the exact level of probability, there is a general acceptance that there is a high probability that an investment portfolio will provide cash payments throughout a 30-year retirement if the retiree draws from that portfolio an amount each year that is in line with the "Bengen Rule." The Bengen Rule states that a retiree, in the first year of retirement, may draw about 4% of the portfolio's value at the beginning of retirement, and each year thereafter, draw the same dollar amount, adjusted only for inflation (irrespective of the portfolio's investment performance).

---

15 "Between the adoption of individual retirement accounts in 1974 and the 401(k) in 1981, the way people planned and invested for retirement began to change. Faced with selecting investments for retirement accounts, the changes caused by the Tax Reform Act in 1986, and a stock market that began to take off in 1982, more people realized they needed help with their financial lives." http://www.thinkadvisor.com/2005/12/01/the-history-of-financial-planning

William Bengen demonstrated this rule in a *Journal of Financial Planning* article in1994, using historical investment performance data. More recently, Monte Carlo testing[16] has shown that a retiree's chances of avoiding portfolio "ruin" are greater than 90% if the retiree follows the Bengen Rule. This approach provides for constant purchasing power across the retirement years and thus takes account of the assumption that inflation will impact spending needs.

Sequence of Returns

The thousands of possible "lifetime" outcomes the planner generates from a Monte Carlo simulation will display more failures (i.e., cash flow exhaustion) if the retiree's retirement plan portfolio encounters an especially bad sequence of investment returns. This phenomenon is particularly dangerous if the bad returns occur in the early years of retirement.

If the early portfolio returns are low or negative, there is long-term impact on the portfolio size. That is especially true if the portfolio funds are used to provide for spending needs during the down period. To illustrate, Thornburg Investment Management prepared a paper describing how the order of portfolio returns on investment can affect portfolio survival:

> *"Sequence of returns is simply the order in which returns are realized by a retiree. The consequences of a bad sequence of returns, especially early in retirement, can mean premature depletion of the portfolio. Retirees need to avoid being in the position of having to sell during inopportune market environments."*

---

16 A Monte Carlo simulation is a mathematical tool that offers a way to evaluate a particular retirement portfolio.With the help of computer software, a planner can simulate hundreds or thousands of market-condition scenarios and learn the probability that your portfolio would last your expected lifetime.

Chart 9.4

S & P 500 Index with Inverted Sequence of Returns

Figure 1. S&P 500 Index Sequence of Returns

Year	1989-2008 Sequence	2008-1989 Sequence
1	31.69	-37.00
2	-3.11	5.49
3	30.47	15.84
4	7.62	4.91
5	10.08	10.88
6	1.32	28.68
7	37.58	-22.10
8	22.96	-11.88
9	33.36	-9.11
10	28.58	21.04
11	21.04	28.58
12	-9.11	33.36
13	-11.88	22.96
14	-22.10	37.58
15	28.68	1.32
16	10.88	10.08
17	4.91	7.62
18	15.84	30.47
19	5.49	-3.11
20	-37.00	31.69
Avg. Annual Return	8.43%	8.43%

Past performance does not guarantee future results.
Source: S&P 500

The "average return for this twenty-year period was 8.43%. Reverse the sequence, 2008–1989, and once again, the average annual return is 8.43%!" In fact, if the portfolio is neither added to nor drawn from during the time period under examination, the order of the returns does not affect the average annual return nor the amount in the portfolio at the end of the time period. However, "for retirees taking systematic withdrawals, the order in which they realize their returns is crucial to the long-term sustainability of the retirement portfolio."

To demonstrate that phenomenon, Thornburg then applied the two different sets of returns, with identical average rates of returns, to a hypothetical portfolio from which the retiree is taking withdrawals. The difference in portfolio values at the end of 20 years is almost $3 million dollars!

Chart 9.5

Sequence of Returns Impact on a Hypothetical $1 Million Investment with Retiree Taking Withdrawals (5% Initial Rate, 3% Inflation) $50,000 first year

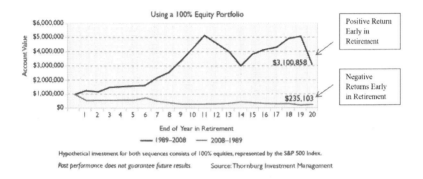

"The portfolio is invested 100% in equities represented by the S&P 500 Index. As you can see from the chart, after 20 years in retirement, the 1989–2008 sequence has supported the retirement spending and allowed the account value to grow to over $3.1 million. However, the results for the 2008–1989 sequence are quite different. The negative 37% performance in year one followed by significant negative returns in years seven, eight, and nine dramatically deteriorated the account value to approximately $235,000 at the end of the 20-year period."

Reverse Dollar Cost Averaging

In the accumulation phase, a client can take advantage of Dollar Cost Averaging by making systematic "buys" for his portfolio. This is what 401(k) participants do when they devote a portion of the paycheck to a "contribution." No matter what the market is doing, the client continues to buy without regard to market values. He is not trying to time the market but is adhering to a **buy and hold** strategy. Over the course of his earning years, he will have paid top dollar for some of his assets when the market was hot. Conversely, he would have bought some of them greatly discounted when the market was in a bear portion of its volatility cycle. Say he is contributing $100 per paycheck. Sometimes that $100 will not buy much, but when the market declines, his $100 will buy him/her more units per dollar invested. At the end of 40 years, his numerous, discounted assets were likely to have risen to normal values and thus contributed significantly to portfolio value over time.

When a client retires and enters the distribution phase, the opposite happens. Now he is "selling" his assets, on a regular schedule, to meet his spending goals. When the market is hot he sells fewer units to raise the money he needs, but in a bear market he must divest more units to meet his needs. This outcome violates a universal rule of investing: buy low and sell high.

A simplified hypothetical example illustrates **Reverse Dollar Cost Averaging**. Mr. and Mrs. Hail were using Uber shares to provide monthly income beyond what their Social Security benefits and small pension contributed. At the beginning of their retirement, their Uber stock shares were selling for $1,000 per share. They needed about $1000 a month. So they sold one share per month, but then the market tanked and the share price declined to $500. They now had to sell *two* shares per month, and once those shares were sold, they were gone for good. They locked in their losses by having no choice but to sell in a bear market.

Over a 30 year retirement, Reverse Dollar Cost Averaging can jeopardize a nest egg. Thornburg demonstrates this effect on a hypothetical portfolio over 5 years. When share prices drop for the **Not Optimal** (on right) portfolio, many more shares have to be sold to raise the $50,000 the retiree needs. Over this period, 31,032 shares were sold due to bear market conditions versus only 23,569 shares sold in the **Optimal** order of returns:

Optimal					Not Optimal			
Year	Share Price	Withdrawal Amount	Shares Sold		Year	Share Price	Withdrawal Amount	Shares Sold
Beginning	$10				Beginning	$10		
1	$10	- $50,000	- 5,000		1	$10	- $50,000	- 5,000
2	$12	- $50,000	- 4,167		2	$6	- $50,000	- 8,333
3	$13	- $50,000	- 3,846		3	$7	- $50,000	- 7,143
4	$9	- $50,000	- 5,556		4	$9	- $50,000	- 5,556
5	$10	- $50,000	- 5,000		5	$10	- $50,000	- 5,000

Initial Share Value	$10.00	
Average Share Price	$10.80	
Total Shares Sold		-23,569

Initial Share Value	$10.00	
Average Share Price	$8.40	
Total Shares Sold		-31,032

The above charts are designed to demonstrate the mathematical principle behind reverse dollar cost averaging. The illustrations are hypothetical and are not intended to serve as a projection of the investment results of any particular investment.

4. Consumption

These questions arise immediately and are easily understood:

A. Will retirees be willing or even able to live comfortably on a budget that limits their spending to a withdrawal rate that is sustainable for 30-40 years?

B. Will retirees adjust to market volatility and scale back consumption when market returns are weak or negative?

How a Reverse Mortgage Can Help Mitigate Risk of Financial Ruin in Retirement

In 2005, Dr. Sacks introduced a new concept in reverse mortgages. In doing so he revamped the way a reverse mortgage could be used. Traditionally, reverse mortgages were left as a last resort, to be considered only if and when a retiree had exhausted his other assets. Dr. Sacks turned this concept on its head. He studied using the reverse mortgage, selectively, during the entire course of retirement. He wanted to avoid unfavorable results from a bad sequence of portfolio returns, and the impact of reverse dollar cost averaging. As we have seen, these phenomena are dangerous to Boomers managing their own retirement income because periods of market volatility are certain to happen during a longer retirement.

Dr. Sacks viewed the house as another asset that could provide income in retirement. Could this asset provide income that could substitute temporarily for portfolio draws? Could a reverse mortgage be used in coordination with portfolio withdrawals throughout retirement? In other words, would the reverse mortgage help protect the client's portfolio in bear markets? (And, Dr. Sacks noted, unlike securities, which generally need to be sold in order to provide income, and hence are gone once they are sold, a reverse mortgage does not diminish the continuing shelter and enjoyment of the home.)

To test his theory, Dr. Sacks compared 5,000 possible outcomes with two identical simulated portfolios, based on historical rates of return. The first portfolio was drawn upon until exhausted. The second portfolio used reverse mortgage credit line draws instead of portfolio draws following bear markets. These reverse mortgage draws enabled the homeowner to avoid having to sell securities when they were undervalued. An example, illustrating the results of this kind of test, is shown in the table below. (Note that the 6.5% Initial Rate is dramatically higher than the typical 4% rate that most planners budget.)

Example 9.1

Integrating Reverse Mortgage in Retirement Distribution over 30 Years $1,000,000 (60%Stock/40% Fixed Income) Portfolio Drawn at 6.5% Initial Rate Draw Adjusted Yearly for Inflation, Initial Home Value $1 Million Appreciating at 4% Historical Market Data, 5,000 Trials

For a client with a $1,000,000 initial portfolio value wanting to start with a $65,000 (6.5%) initial draw:

Draw Source	Remaining Portfolio	Remaining Net Worth *Including* Housing Wealth
Portfolio until exhausted, Then Reverse Mortgage When and if Portfolio is exhausted	$0/ 35% of trials	Range : $600,000 to $12 million
Portfolio, except Reverse Mortgage Following years with Bad Investment Returns	$0 /14% of trials	Range : $1.1 to 13.9 million

The interesting conclusion to draw from these examples is the following:

> *"The use of the Coordinated Strategy generally increases the mean value of the retiree's overall net worth at later times, even though the home equity may be lower than it might be if the Coordinated Strategy is not used."*

> *Barry H. Sacks,*
> *"A RETIREMENT INCOME STRATEGY FOR*
> *MODERATELY AFFLUENT RETIREES."*

Summary

Results from his initial investigation suggested to Dr. Sacks that more research needed to be done. Rather than rely on establishing a reverse mortgage after the portfolio is exhausted, it appeared that a better use would be to set up a reverse mortgage *early* in retirement and then draw from it strategically, only when portfolio returns did not provide the needed pay out. What happened next changed the illiquid house into an asset termed "housing wealth."

CHAPTER 10

How Can Reverse Mortgage Funds Be Distributed for Greater Retirement Security?

I n 2012, Dr. Sacks and his brother Stephen R. Sacks, Ph.D. (a retired professor of economics) published an article in the *Journal
of Financial Planning* expanding the original theory and demonstrating that coordinating housing wealth via a reverse mortgage
significantly increases cash flow survival probability throughout
retirement. A few months later, **John Salter, Ph.D., CFP®, AIFA®;
Shaun Pfeiffer; and Harold Evensky, CFP®, AIF® of Texas Tech
University** published an article in the same journal. Although they
took a slightly different approach, their conclusions validated the
Sacks' results: using a reverse mortgage as a Standby Line of credit
(accessing it to substitute for portfolio draws when the market is
down), is a powerful cash flow survival tool. Since 2012, other investigators have published case studies demonstrating that a reverse
mortgage, distributed in various methods, can play a key role in
retirement planning.

The HECM reverse mortgage is available in a range of configurations:

1. A Lump Sum

2. A Term Payment

3. A Tenure Payment

4. A Line of Credit

5. A Combination

6. A Future Change in Distribution

Lump Sum

The client may choose to take an initial lump sum if he meets certain requirements known as **mandatory obligations**. He will be assessed a higher Upfront MIP rate (2.5% versus .5%) if he takes the lump sum before Day 366. We have seen that the lump sum can be used in this fashion to purchase a new principal residence (HECM for Purchase).

Others have found that they could start a second career by funding their capital needs with a HECM. That they are not making payments can translate into a competitive advantage as they build the business. Once they have established cash flow, they can pay down/off the HECM without penalty.

The most common lump sum disbursal involves replacing a current mortgage with a HECM. With a HECM replacement, monthly household debt payment is reduced. Analysts are interested in how replacing debt with a HECM can affect a retiree's securities portfolio in retirement. Calculators are available online, for example at www.financinglongevity.com, to help illustrate whether or not replacing a regular mortgage with a HECM could improve portfolio conservation.

For example, at age 66, when Mrs. Connelly's husband died, she was saddled with a mortgage she could not afford. Her home was a mecca for family gatherings so she did not want to move out of her neighborhood, far away from her grandchildren. She did have a $750,000 nest egg but her current expenses were $6,000 a month, including $1200 in principal and interest payments on her mortgage. Her planner understood her predicament and suggested that she replace her mortgage with a HECM.

The adviser was able to demonstrate that if her portfolio returned 6% yearly for the remainder of her life, her spending (including her mortgage payments, and with her other expenses adjusted for inflation at 3% yearly) would exhaust the portfolio by the time she reached age 89. If, however, she replaced the mortgage with a reverse mortgage, thus reducing her initial spending needs to $4,800 a month, her portfolio, under the same assumptions, would not be exhausted, and instead would be worth $115,873 when she reached age 100. (This projection does not account for market volatility. In reality, no diversified securities portfolio yields a steady rate of return year after year. Nonetheless, it provides a useful illustration.)

Chart 10.1

www.financinglongevity.com

Of course, the foregoing comparisons favor the outcome using the reverse mortgage because an otherwise unused asset has been put to work to reduce monthly expenses. So in a sense, they are "apples to oranges" comparisons. A more helpful comparison, more directly "apples to apples," is the comparison between the cash flow survival probability when the reverse mortgage is used in a coordinated manner (as described by either the Sacks' or by Prof. Salter et al) and the cash flow survival probability when the reverse mortgage is considered and used only as a last resort.

Every lender can provide a schedule displaying the effect of the reverse mortgage on retained equity. Below is an example of an amortization schedule for a borrower taking a monthly payment of $1,217.84 a month for a 20-year term. A $100,000 Line of Credit remains. The amortization illustrates how the loan balance grows, how the LOC grows, and what the remaining equity in the property would be if rates remained low.

Chart 10.2

Sample Amortization Schedule (First 10 years of 20 year Term $14,614.08/year)

Amortization Schedule - Annual Projections

Borrower Name/Case Number:	Sample, Knoll		Refinance:	No
Age of Youngest Borrower:	66	Initial Property Value:	$500,000.00
Int. Rate (Expected / Initial):	5.11% / 3.63%	Beg. Mortgage Balance:	$461.25
Maximum Claim Amount:	$500,000.00	Expected Appreciation:	4.00%
Initial Principal Limit:	$266,036.75	Initial Line of Credit:	$100,000.00
Initial Advance:	$0.00	Monthly Payment:	$1,217.84
Lien Payoffs with Reverse Mortgage:	$0.00	Monthly Service Fee:	$0.00
Financed Closing Costs:	$461.25	Mortgage Insurance (MIP):	1.25%

NOTE: Actual interest charges and property value projections may vary from amounts shown. Available credit will be less than projected if funds withdrawn from line-of-credit.

			Annual Totals					End of Year Projections			
Yr	Age	SVC Fee	Cash Payment	Credit Draw	MIP	Rate	Interest	Loan Balance	Line Of Credit	Property Value	Equity
0	66	$0.00	$0.00	$0.00	$0.00	3.63%	$0.00	$461.25	$100,000.00	$500,000.00	$499,538.75
1	67	$0.00	$14,614.08	$0.00	$106.34	3.63%	$308.46	$15,490.12	$104,986.46	$520,000.00	$504,509.88
2	68	$0.00	$14,614.08	$0.00	$298.45	3.63%	$865.75	$31,268.40	$110,221.57	$540,800.00	$509,531.60
3	69	$0.00	$14,614.08	$0.00	$500.15	3.63%	$1,450.83	$47,833.48	$115,717.72	$582,432.00	$514,598.54
4	70	$0.00	$14,614.08	$0.00	$711.90	3.63%	$2,065.09	$65,224.53	$121,487.94	$584,929.28	$519,704.75
5	71	$0.00	$14,614.08	$0.00	$934.22	3.63%	$2,709.97	$83,482.80	$127,545.89	$608,326.45	$524,843.65
6	72	$0.00	$14,614.08	$0.00	$1,167.61	3.63%	$3,387.01	$102,651.51	$133,905.91	$632,659.51	$530,008.00
7	73	$0.00	$14,614.08	$0.00	$1,412.65	3.63%	$4,097.82	$122,776.06	$140,583.08	$657,965.89	$535,189.83
8	74	$0.00	$14,614.08	$0.00	$1,669.91	3.63%	$4,844.06	$143,904.11	$147,593.20	$684,284.53	$540,380.42
9	75	$0.00	$14,614.08	$0.00	$1,939.99	3.63%	$5,627.52	$166,085.70	$154,952.87	$711,655.91	$545,570.21
10	76	$0.00	$14,614.08	$0.00	$2,223.54	3.63%	$6,450.05	$189,373.37	$162,679.53	$740,122.14	$550,748.77

Term Payment

Sometimes a family may need to extract as much money per month from their HECM as they can in order to pay for in-home health care. The HECM allows for a term payment. Once the term is up there are no more draws allowed, but the loan stays in place until the last participating borrower dies, moves, or sells.

In 2002, Mr. and Mrs. Weinstein lived in an expensive Bethesda, Maryland home. They faced significant bills when they chose to keep Mr. Weinstein at home as he struggled with a life-ending illness. They needed as much money per month as they could access to fund his care. Mrs. Weinstein was quite a bit younger than her husband, so she elected to go off title to allow them to use his birthdate to calculate the available funds. The HECM term plan easily met this $8,000 a month cost and in this case, the term did last until Mr. Weinstein died.

This was an interesting case because Mrs. Weinstein had "gone off title." (Today's HUD rules will not allow a scenario like this.) After Mr. Weinstein died, she would have to arrange her own financing to settle the HECM debt, or move. Luckily, this couple has an adept financial planner. There was a life insurance policy in place to help Mrs. Weinstein. She elected to sell the Bethesda house, and retain the remaining equity. She moved to their vacation home in Boca Raton and used the sale proceeds from the Bethesda property and the money from the insurance policy to strengthen her retirement.

Tenure Payment: A Floor

Sometimes a homeowner just wants to know that he will be receiving a dependable stream of mailbox money, every month for as long as he lives. The Tenure Payment option allows the borrower to "annuitize" his home equity. Rather than use cash to purchase an annuity, the HECM borrower uses his housing wealth to accomplish this purpose. By using housing wealth to purchase this annuity, more of his assets stay invested , producing investment returns. This strategy achieves more time in the market, a planning mantra. And of course, while the housing wealth is used to purchase the annuity, the homeowner still retains the full shelter and enjoyment of the house.

Caution: A HECM annuity differs from a traditional annuity in another important aspect. The housing annuity (tenure payment) ends when the last borrower leaves the house permanently. A HECM annuity payment is not portable. This is an important feature to consider if a client's other resources are limited. Also of note is that a HECM annuity and other annuities can coexist. Using a traditional annuity does not prevent a homeowner from using a HECM, as well.[17]

---

17 If a homeowner is planning to use HECM funds to *purchase* a commercial annuity, extra disclosures are required at application.

Note, however, that ending a traditional annuity early means forfeiting the original investment. This cannot happen with a HECM. If the borrower sets up a tenure payment and either dies early or termi-nates the annuity, the remaining equity is still intact and belongs to the homeowner or his or her heirs.

Mr. and Mrs. Graves of Philadelphia wanted to supplement their retirement income with a monthly guaranteed payment. They were able to create a monthly annuity from their home of $1,715.39 based on an initial credit limit (Principal Limit) of $295,500 on a $500,000 property. In doing so, they were able to leave a $240,000 brokerage account invested. As long as one of them was living in the house as a principal residence, this payment arrived month after month , year after year . They liked the security of knowing that they had baseline income, a floor below which their revenue stream provided by Social Security, and by their house, would not fall. There are numerous calculators online that will illustrate how keeping that $240,000 could provide returns to help finance retirement.

Chart 10.3

$240,000 Performance in Market at 6% Annual Return

Results Summary	
Starting amount	$240,000.00
Years	20 years.
Additional contributions	$0.00 per month
Rate of return	6% compounded annually
Total amount you will have contributed	$240,000.00
Total interest	$529,712.55
Total at end of investment	$769,712.55

http://www.dinkytown.net/java/CompoundSavings.html

In this hypothetical example the Graves household was able to stay invested and watch their $240,000 grow to $769,000. Again, this is an "apple to oranges" comparison because the HECM will accrue interest and reduce housing equity. The portfolio grew but debt on the house grew as well. What is that cost?

All HECM lenders can produce an amortization schedule pre-dicting what the cost of the HECM reverse mortgage would be over the same term (**Chart 10.2**).Whether or not it makes sense to use a HECM to allow a borrower to retain his portfolio longer includes assessing the cost of depleting home equity to do so. For those with a bequest motive, it is important to ask whether or not the heirs would prefer inheriting a house, or an investment portfolio. The answer to this may depend on how unified the heirs are on selling the house and dividing those proceeds.

Dr. Gerald Wagner, a Harvard Ph.D. and an expert in both reverse mortgages and portfolio theory, published a paper in the *Journal of Financial Planning*, December, 2013, investigating how tenure payment supplements can provide greater spending success, particularly in higher tax rate locales. For a 63-year-old borrower living in a $450,000 home and having an $800,000 retirement portfolio, if the first year's withdrawal need is 6.0 %, the amount withdrawn is $48,000, *i.e.*, $4,000 a month. His analysis showed:

> *"After paying federal and California taxes, this leaves the homeowner with $2,583 to spend. If the client chooses a HECM tenure payment, there is $1,328 tax-free each month from the HECM. On a tax equivalent basis, that is $2,057, so to meet the desired portfolio withdrawal of $4,000, only $1,943 needs to be withdrawn from the portfolio each month during the first year. Because the HECM tenure advance is fixed, the monthly portfolio withdrawal in the second year will be $2,043. The $100 increase over the first year accounts for the 2.5 % expected annual inflation."*

> *"Depending on the relative values of the home and portfolio, withdrawal rates of 5.0 % to 6.0 % can be achieved with **over a 90 % chance of success over 30 years**."*

For retirees unable to budget at an initial withdrawal rate of 4% (or less), supplementing with a reverse mortgage may provide enough additional income so that their spending needs are met and their portfolio is sufficiently protected to survive for 30 years or more.

Line of Credit: A Back Up Plan in Retirement

When a homeowner establishes a HECM as a Line of Credit (LOC), he is gaining access to his housing wealth to be available at any time in the future. (Drawing all the funds before the Day 366 will cause a higher MIP assessment.) This LOC has a truly unusual and remarkable feature: The amount available to be borrowed (to the extent not yet borrowed) grows each month. The rate at which the amount of the LOC not yet borrowed grows is equal to the sum of the monthly interest rate charged on any loan balance outstanding (most servicers require a minimum loan balance of $50) PLUS 1/12 of the ongoing MIP rate (now 1.25%, or .104 a month). This feature cannot be canceled; it is a contractual obligation made by the lender to the borrower, and insured by the FHA.

As explained by Dr. Wagner in his December, 2013 *Journal of Financial Planning* article, "The growing line-of-credit feature maintains the borrowing capacity regardless of when the mortgage is accessed.

> "For example, with a note rate of 2.50 percent and an on-going MIP of 1.25 percent per annum, a loan's effect rate would be 3.75 Percent. Imagine two borrowers , each with an initial $100,000 line of credit. One draws his entire line of credit at the end of the first year; after one year the capacity would have grown [with monthly compounding] to $103,815. The other borrower lets her line of credit capacity grow untouched for five years. After five years, the first borrower would owe $120,588. That is $103,815 in principal and $16,773 in accrued interest and MIP. The second borrower could owe nothing and have a line-of-credit capacity of $120,588. If she then withdrew her whole line of credit, both borrowers would have exactly the same outstanding loan balance."[18]

---

18 *http://www.onefpa.org/journal/Pages/December-2013-The-6-0-Percent-Rule. aspx*

The growing HECM LOC impressed Dr. John Salter and Harold Evensky, CFP®, of Texas Tech University, for these reasons:

1. The HECM LOC cannot be canceled

2. The HECM LOC cannot be frozen

3. The HECM LOC cannot be reduced

4. The HECM LOC will grow in value even if the housing value drops

Dr. Salter, and Harold Evensky, known as the "Dean of Financial Planning," along with Dr. Shaun Pfeiffer, began a series of studies on how the HECM LOC could function as a Standby LOC to meet volatility challenges throughout retirement. All lenders are equipped to provide amortization schedules illustrating anticipated LOC growth. These schedules, however, cannot provide a totally accurate prediction of LOC growth because it is not possible to predict what interest rates will be in the future. Because HECMs with the LOC feature use adjustable rates, from month to month, or year to year, the loan balance will be charged a varying rate. Interested borrowers may wish to request multiple amortization schedules over a range of potential future interest rates. The borrower can choose either yearly adjusting rates or monthly adjusting rates.

Chart 10.3

Compounding Growth of HECM LOC v. Home Value

The higher the rate charged on the loan balance, however, the faster the HECM LOC will grow:

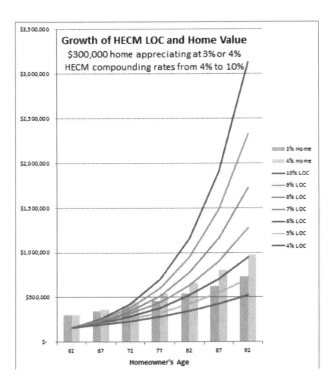

Thomas C. B. Davison, MA, PhD, CFP®, illustrates how the LOC compounds. If interest rates rise over the course of the loan, the LOC would, in time, outstrip the value of the house if housing values rise at a typical 3 or 4% annually.[19]

Combination

Homeowners may combine two or more configurations. For example, a borrower with a $225,000 initial credit capacity may take $50,000 in a lump sum, $500 a month on a 7 year term in order

---

to avoid taking an early Social Security benefit, and leave the rest in a growing LOC.

A Future Change in Distribution

A fixed-rate HECM requires a full lump sum draw when the loan is consummated. This results in zero access to future draws. The payout options, however, are not locked in with adjustable rate HECMs.

Most loan servicers will charge the loan balance a nominal fee ($25) to rearrange how an adjustable rate HECM is distributed. It is possible, for example, to convert a tenure payment to a LOC, and back. The calculation is based, in the background, on what the original Principal Limit (credit capacity) has grown to be, and the current age of the youngest participant. The original Expected Rate used at loan's inception is applied to determine a conversion from the LOC to tenure payments.

For example, a client may start with tenure payments, and then decide to slow his housing consumption, and debt, by switching to a LOC. The payments will cease and whatever available credit is left "flows" into the LOC. The LOC will grow monthly. Years later the client may want to resume monthly tenure payments. The current LOC, the original Expected Rate, and the age of the youngest eligible participant will determine how much those monthly payments will be.

The new tenure payment could be quite high due to advanced age, and the large LOC from which the payment will be calculated. This effect is accentuated if interest rates were low at loan inception (a bigger credit limit), but rose to a higher rate over the years. These phenomena would cause accelerated growth on a larger initial LOC, resulting in a higher payment.

Conclusion

The HECM program is flexible and, as long as the credit capacity is not exhausted, it allows the borrower to mix and match different payment options. Over the term, the homeowner can adjust his payments to reflect current needs. More money either left in, or returned to, the Line of Credit results in greater equity access for future needs, especially if interest rates rise. Despite what some television financial advisers claim, it is best to set up a reverse mortgage while interest rates are low. The initial available credit will be at its highest, and future growth in the LOC will benefit from rising interest rates over time.

CHAPTER 11

Breaking News: Latest Research on How Home Equity Helps Other Assets

Most investors immediately comprehend the wisdom of diversifying assets. It's as easy as some wisdom that you learned in kindergarten: Don't keep all your eggs in one basket. Yet, investigators have noted that the housing asset represents an enormous **undiversified** asset. Owners tend to treat the house as a sacred cow even though its value is solely dependent on the local housing market. By electing to use the asset for other purposes, even if only to initiate a Standby Line of Credit, owners can convert the asset to an insurance policy, for example, or substitute it for taxable income. In doing so, benefits not normally associated with housing wealth may improve the homeowner's overall financial security. And this improvement is realized without any loss of the shelter and enjoyment of the home.

Tax Equivalents

There is growing interest in the HECM by portfolio theorists and other academicians, in part because of tax considerations. When a client borrows money from his house via a Home Equity Line of Credit (HELOC), the draws from that loan are not treated as income for tax purposes. Likewise, proceeds from a HECM loan are not treated as income for tax purposes.

Therefore, drawing from the HECM LOC may have tax advantages over other forms of cash flow during retirement.

In the *Journal of Financial Planning*, Gerald Wagner, PhD, noted in his paper *The 6% Solution:*

> "For example, a 63-year-old borrower with $250,000 available for a payment plan could receive $1,449 each month from a HECM tenure plan; that is $17,387 per year, and because these are nontaxable loan advances, the payment's tax equivalent value is considerably higher. If the marginal federal bracket was 28.0 %, and the borrower lived in California (10.3 % tax rate), the tax equivalent value of these tenure advances would be $26,740."[20]

For this client, drawing home equity at the rate of $17,387 is the equivalent of having drawn $26,740 from his portfolio. **Thomas C. B. Davison, MA, PhD, CFP®,** discovered the same tax advantage in using home equity when compared to portfolio draws (private correspondence):

> "The way to figure out what you can spend is first to figure out what the tax is, then subtract that from the withdrawal, and spend what's left. If the tax rate is 33%, then the tax on $1.50 is $1.50 x0.33, which is $0.49.5, leaving you $1.00 to spend after a bit of rounding. Or in fractions: the tax is (1/3)x$1.50 = $1.50/3, or 50 cents."

For every dollar spent in home equity, that is $1.50 not withdrawn from the portfolio.

Tax Bracket Creep

Others have noted that substituting draws from a reverse mortgage to avoid large draws from other assets may prevent triggering a higher tax rate. For example, Wade D. Pfau, PhD, CFA, Professor

20 *http://www.onefpa.org/journal/Pages/The%206.0%%20Rule.aspx*

of Retirement Income, The American College wrote: *"Proceeds from a reverse mortgage or from the cash value of life insurance could also be used in such a way to boost spending without increasing taxable income."*[21]

Understanding How Interest Payments on HECM Loans Can Be Deducted

People who plan to use their HECM as a revolving line of credit want to know how payments on the loan balance can qualify for mortgage interest deductions. Of course, mortgage interest is only deductible when paid. Reverse mortgages are treated the same way as traditional forward mortgages; mortgage interest is deductible, but only when paid, not just accrued. Because the HECM loan balance increases at not only the interest rate but the MIP rate as well, care must be taken to determine how much of the total amount owed is interest and hence can be deducted:

- The ongoing 1.25% Mortgage Insurance Premium (MIP) is not considered interest, although it is part of the compounding rate. The interest charge is the sum of the variable component (LIBOR) and the lender's margin.

- If the borrower does not make payments on mortgage until the loan ends, all the interest will be paid off as a lump sum, resulting in a large deduction in one year. The deduction may be larger than the taxable income in that year! It may be on the estate tax return if the home is sold and mortgage paid off after death.

- As the monthly addition to the loan balance is both MIP and interest, not all of it will be deductible.
  - "If you currently have a HECM reverse mortgage, then your payments are applied in the following order: first to that part of your loan balance representing mortgage insurance premiums, secondly to that part of your loan balance

21 *http://blogs.wsj.com/experts/2015/03/19/how-to-increase-your-after-tax-wealth-in-retirement/*

representing servicing fees, thirdly to that part of your loan balance representing interest charges, and finally to that part of your loan balance representing principal advances. The National Reverse Mortgage Lenders Association strongly advises that you confirm with your loan servicer the manner in which your partial prepayments will be applied to your specific account." (NRMLA, 2014)

o A payment will at most be partially deductible. Any payment less than the currently accumulated MIP and servicing fees would not be deductible. Note that the interest component of the monthly compounding rate will be larger than the MIP and servicing fees—typically a much larger fraction, especially as interest rates rise.

o In the Standby Reverse Mortgage scenario used by Salter et al. all the money borrowed in market downturns was paid back when markets recovered, so all the interest paid during that market downturn would be deductible.[22]

The Lost Tax Deduction for Estate Planning

As a result of a conversation with loan officer Nick Maningas of Philadelphia, Dr. Barry H. Sacks investigated the effect of taking a deduction of the accumulated interest from a reverse mortgage to offset the income tax due from the borrower's heir(s) following the borrower's death:

> *The use of the reverse mortgage results in accrued interest. Because the interest is accrued, but is not actually paid, by the borrower, the borrower does not have an income tax deduction for that interest. The interest deduction seems to be "lost". However, that deduction can be recovered by the borrower's beneficiary (or beneficiaries) in the following way: 401(k) accounts and rollover IRAs are among the few assets that, when left to beneficiaries, subject the*

---

22 *Thomas C. B. Davison, MA, PhD, CFP*, www.toolsforretirementplanning. com*

beneficiaries to income tax. Some or all of that income tax can be eliminated by the use of the following simple technique (by which the beneficiary gets an interest deduction to offset some or all of the income from the rollover IRA or 401(k) account):Be sure that the decedent's home, which is subject to the reverse mortgage debt, goes <u>directly</u> to the same heir (or heirs) who is (or are) the beneficiary (or beneficiaries) of the decedent's 401(k) account or rollover IRA, <u>and</u> be sure that the home becomes a "qualified residence" (as defined in the Internal Revenue Code) of the heir (or heirs) <u>before</u> it is sold. (The conventional approach to dealing with the assets would be to have the estate sell the home and distribute the proceeds. The approach described is different from the conventional approach, and may need to be written into the client's will or trust.) Private Correspondence[23]

Tax-Free Way to Fund Other Financial Products?

There are no restrictions on how HECM funds are used. It is possible to use tax-free HECM draws to fund existing insurance policies, or create new ones. Beneficiaries, of course, receive life insurance proceeds tax-free.

Some advisers view the compounding growth in the HECM Line of Credit as a way of self insuring for long term care. If the long term care expense never materializes, the client has lost nothing by setting up the fund but has certainly hedged against the possibility that future health care needs could otherwise drain assets.

As a caution, clients considering using housing wealth to purchase Long Term Insurance, however, are advised to make sure that the policy premiums can be sustained until the care is needed. In *Falling Short: The Coming Retirement Crisis*, authors Charles D. Ellis, Alicia H. Munnell, and Andrew D. Eschtruth,

---

23 *Private correspondence with author*

"...strongly favor a catastrophic policy with premiums paid up front. This product would pay for benefits only after the individual has paid, for say, 12 months of nursing home care, or $80,000. This arrangement would change an unbounded black hole of expense into a known quantity. Moreover, the premium for this benefit would be relatively modest and could be paid in single lump sum at retirement so buyers need not worry about premium costs climbing as they age. The hope would be that once people understood the dimensions for their exposure to long-term care costs, they would feel more comfortable about spending their balances and tapping their home equity. Unfortunately, such a product does not currently exist in the United States."

Roth Conversion Taxes

If the portfolio must be tapped to pay taxes on a Roth IRA conversion, some advisers suggest using a draw from a reverse mortgage to cover the tax bite. The advantage of this approach is that it uses untaxed money to pay the tax on the conversion. Using money from the traditional IRA itself would reduce the remaining IRA amount. For example, if the taxpayer is in the 30% tax bracket, and converts a $100,000 traditional IRA, paying the tax with money from the IRA, the remaining IRA amount, in the Roth IRA, will be $70,000. If, instead, the taxpayer uses a reverse mortgage credit line draw to pay the tax, there will be $100,000 in the Roth IRA. Growth in a Roth IRA is not taxable.

Deferring Social Security Using the HECM as an Income Bridge

The media continue to highlight strategies on to how maximize social security benefits. Many people would like to defer taking benefits until age 70 because of the substantial increase in benefits earned with that delay.[24] Chart 11.1 demonstrates that a delay in taking benefits results in a much higher monthly payment.

Chart 11.1

Social Security Benefits by Age

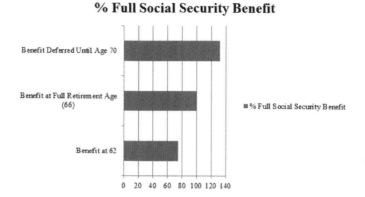

The problem with waiting until age 70 is giving up income in those years from 62-70 until qualifying for the maximum payout at 70. Thomas C. B. Davison, MA, PhD, CFP® published a case study on his blog, *www.toolsforretirementplanning.com*, in which the client uses home equity for income during many of the deferral years. The survival probability for the client's plan improved from 5% to 90%. This case illustrates how a homeowner could use a reverse mortgage to fund her needs for the first 6 years. Once the HECM funds are exhausted, she relies on her portfolio. But at age 70, she is able to reduce her portfolio draws because she is getting the largest possible social security benefit. Interestingly, the reasons her plan showed such improvement in financial stability are not just related to getting a higher social security benefit at 70:

- This client's reverse mortgage funded 6+ years of spending.

- She had more assets to spend because she added $240,000 in home wealth to her $500,000 IRA.

---

24 *For an overview of social security claiming strategies, see Mary Beth Franklin at: http://www.investmentnews.com/section/retirement2*

- Taxes matter: This client was in the 33%+ tax bracket, State/Federal combined. The Reverse Mortgage was tax-free so every $1.00 draw has the spending power of $1.50 drawn from the IRA. In total, the $240,000 spent from her Reverse Mortgage was the equivalent of $360,000 of IRA funds.

- The investment portfolio was untouched for an extra 6 years. Keeping the portfolio invested reduces chances that she will encounter a bad sequence of returns early in retirement.

- At age 70, she enjoys the highest Social Security benefits possible, further reducing portfolio draws in her later years.

Chart 11.2

Portfolio Comparison Using HECM to Fund Deferral Years

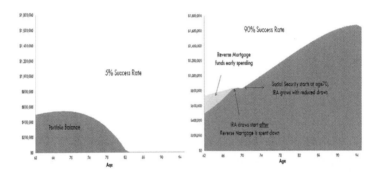

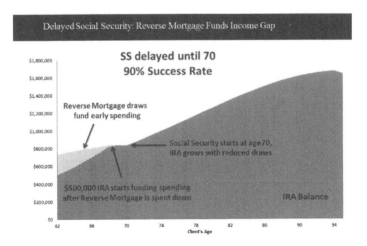

The HECM as a Hedge Against Inflation

Dr. Jack Guttentag has been a vocal HECM proponent for years on his Web site.[25] Dr. Guttentag is a Professor Emeritus at the University of Pennsylvania Wharton School of Business. Never one to mince words, Dr. Guttentag states:

> *"The HECM reverse mortgage is one of the best engineered financial tools of our generation, designed to meet a wide spectrum of senior needs, from repairing the roof of their home, to paying for their grandchildren's education, to meeting expected and unexpected contingencies. Yet the program elicits negative reactions from large segments of the media, whose distorted descriptions of the HECM program are scaring off millions of seniors whose lives could be enriched by it."*

He recommends that retirees establish a HECM Line of Credit early enough to enjoy compounding growth for many years:

> *"The use of the HECM reverse mortgage program as a type of insurance policy employs the credit line feature of the program. The senior uses her borrowing power to draw the largest line available, and lets the line sit unused until she needs it. The longer the senior lives, the longer the credit line sits unused, and the larger it becomes. While her financial assets are gradually being depleted, her credit line is getting larger. She draws on the line if she needs the money, otherwise the equity in her house will pass to her estate.*

> *Why the urgency? The size of the initial HECM credit lines that can be drawn are inversely related to interest rates, while the growth rate of existing unused lines is directly related to rates. Hence, a senior with a specified amount of equity gets the **maximum insurance coverage by taking out the HECM while interest rates are still low, and letting it sit unused as rates rise in the future.**"*

---

25 *www.mtgprofessor.com*

Initial Homeowner Equity of $200,000

Initial Line Effective Rate 5%	Rate on ARM Over 30 Years	Unused Line After 10 Years	Unused Line After 20 Years	Unused Line After 30 Years
$97,800	5%	$177,700	$381,400	**$618,200**
$97,800	6%	$195,300	$402,400	**$829,100**
$97,800	7%	$214,600	$488,400	**$1,111,300**
$97,800	8%	$235,600	$592,100	**$1,487,100**
$97,800	9%	$258,300	$716,800	**$1,989,900**
$97,800	10%	$282,300	$865,000	**$2,650, 400**

In this case, for example, the client begins with a $97,800 HECM Line of Credit. If left untouched for 20 years, she would have access to $402,400 if her line had grown at 6%.[26]

Divorce

A client can buy out his or her spouse by taking a reverse mortgage lump sum on the house. The client can continue to live in the house without having to sell in order to provide the spouse half of the home's value.

If the departing spouse then wishes to buy his own new principal residence, he can use the cash from the reverse mortgage to use as a down payment for a HECM for Purchase transaction.

Or, the marital house can be sold, the proceeds divided. Each spouse can then use that money as a down payment on a separate house and use the HECM Reverse for Purchase for leverage to buy two homes comparable to the original one.

The HECM as a Hedge Against Declining Home Values

Wade D. Pfau, PhD, CFA, Professor of Retirement Income, The American College of Financial Services, published an article in *Advisor Perspectives* demonstrating that establishing a HECM Line of Credit early provides a hedge against home values dropping:

---

26 http://mtgprofessor.com/A%20-%20Reverse%20Mortgages/avoid_outliving_your_money_by_taking_a_HECM_reverse_mortgage_now.html

"With the current HECM rules, those living in their homes long enough could reap a large windfall when the line of credit exceeds the home's value. This potential windfall is amplified by today's low interest rates. Even if the value of the home declines, the line of credit will continue to grow without regard for the home's subsequent value. Combining this with the fact that a HECM is a non-recourse loan means that the HECM provides a very valuable hedging property for home prices."[27]

Conclusion

The notion that the house should never be used to fund retirement except in the most dire circumstances is dying. The last resort strategy was never subjected to any thoughtful and quantitative analysis; the financial world just blindly accepted that a reverse mortgage "should" only be used when all other assets were exhausted. When this approach was subjected to the bright light of mathematics, it became clear that there was no reason to continue advocating a "wait and pray" approach. This is especially true now that academicians fully understand how the HECM Line of Credit compounds over the course of retirement. Recent research treats the HECM as an alternative asset that can be used in concert with other sources of income, often with a synergistic effect.

---

27 http://www.advisorperspectives.com/newsletters14/Hidden_Value_of_Reverse_Mortgage_Standby_Line_of_Credit.php

CHAPTER 12

Who Is the New
HECM Client?

As we have noted, the HECM has changed significantly over time. Accordingly the typical reverse mortgage borrower looks very different than those in the past.

Although the National Reverse Mortgage Lenders Association reports that there is $3.84 TRILLION dollars of home equity owned by Americans 62 and older, one "in four Medicare recipients has less than $12,250 in home equity," according to a new report by the Kaiser Family Foundation, a healthcare non-profit.

Kaiser's calculations also show that the distribution of home equity among older Americans is – like the distribution of income and financial assets – top heavy. While 5% of Medicare beneficiaries in 2013 had more than $398,500 in home equity, half have less than $66,700. According to Kaiser's projections, that gap will widen in the future:

> "By 2030, those whose home equity places them in the top 5% will see that equity grow more than 40%, but it will rise less than 10% for those with mid-level—or median—amounts of equity."[28]

---

28 http://squaredawayblog.bc.edu/squared-away/1-in-4-seniors-have-little-home-equity/

The sad truth is that reverse mortgages will not substantially help the homeowners with few financial resources. Unfortunately, these folks had been targeted inappropriately in the past. Homeowners who could not, or would not, meet their tax and insurance obligations were encouraged to consume all of their reverse mortgage credit in one huge draw.

Actually, the full-draw choice was the only available option for many of these clients. Thousands of older Americans had been caught up in the frenzied housing bubble and had already compromised their equity with subprime, high LTV loans. In order to participate in a reverse mortgage, they had no choice but to take a full lump sum draw to replace their high LTV existing loans with a HECM. When these borrowers failed to meet their tax and insurance obligations, foreclosure was the only option.

In the meantime, housing values collapsed. The insurance fund at the FHA was stressed by having to make good on underwater loans. With his typically blunt style, in "Reverse Mortgage Borrowers Will Have to Prove They Are Not Deadbeats," Dr. Jack Guttentag writes:

> *"One of the attractive features of the HECM reverse mortgage has been that there are no income or credit requirements. All homeowners 62 and older who live in their homes without a mortgage have been eligible, and those with mortgages may also be eligible if the balance is not too large. But all that will change when a series of drastic new FHA rules come into play.*
>
> *The precipitating factor underlying the new rules is the marked rise that has occurred in recent years in property tax defaults by HECM borrowers. While such borrowers are violating their obligations under the reverse mortgage contract, and are thereby subject to foreclosure and eviction, FHA has been understandably reluctant to allow elderly homeowners to be thrown into the street. Instead, FHA has elected to impose income and credit requirements on*

future applicants. The purpose is to assure that henceforth borrowers will have both the capacity and the willingness to pay their property taxes and homeowners insurance."[29]

Always mindful of the ultimate bequest to heirs, Michael Kitces, MSFS, MTAX, CFP®, CLU, ChFC, RHU, REBC, CASL does point out:

"In essence, the intention of the new rules is to shift reverse mortgages from being used as a last resort, to being used more proactively and earlier in the retirement process as a part of a coherent strategy; in other words, as a part of a more comprehensive financial planning approach."[30]

Conclusion

Past events have highlighted how important it is to consume housing wealth prudently, and with an eye to future needs. If staying in the home will stretch a homeowner's ability to meet tax, insurance, and maintenance obligations, today's HECM is not an appropriate choice. The evolution of the HECM, much of which is has been a result of changes adopted by HUD to protect the FHA fund, means that the likely beneficiaries are now middle to upper middle class households. In restructuring how the loan unfolds, HUD has returned the HECM to Congress' original intent. The loan exists to help homeowners mobilize home equity throughout the distribution phase, to help fund a safe, more financially secure retirement. Investigators in the field describe today's ideal client as having invested assets somewhere in the range of $300,000 to $2,000,000, **and** a house.

A borrower who is using a reverse mortgage as a discretionary tool may want to consider an **exit strategy** should interest rates rise substantially. This could involve electing to make payments

---

29 http://www.mtgprofessor.com/A%20-%20Reverse%20Mortgages/
new_income_and_credit_requirements_for_HECM_borrowers.html

30 https://www.kitces.com/blog/will-new-reverse-mortgage-changes-make-
them-a-better-financial-planning-tool/

during high interest rate years in order to keep the loan balance low. Or it could mean paying the balance down. Don't forget that any payments result in a Line of Credit increase that will be there for possible future use. Generally it does not make sense to pay off a reverse mortgage completely, although there are no prepayment penalties. A low balance of just $50 is all it takes to keep the mortgage in force and the Line of Credit growing. The costs of maintaining such a low balance is *de minimis*, yet the utility of having rapid access to the growing Line of Credit could be significant. As Jeff Brown of *Main Street* noted, "Imagine having a retirement safety net that cost nothing to maintain and actually grew as you aged rather than getting smaller. How would that affect other parts of your financial plan?"

CHAPTER 13

How Do I Discuss This with My Financial Adviser?

As Americans move into retirement, they want to feel confident that their nest eggs will last as long as they do. At the same time, they don't want to live on such a strict budget that they cannot enjoy life. Many Americans rely on financial advisers of various stripes to guide them through the saving stage into the spending phase.

Most planners have had no formal training on either reverse mortgages or the protective role that housing wealth can play in volatile markets. This is beginning to change somewhat. The American College of Financial Services, for example, offers a designation, the Retirement Income Certified Professional (RICP®), which provides advisers with a comprehensive view of retirement income planning. Part of that curriculum addresses housing and housing wealth, including reverse mortgage mechanics and strategies. According to the RICP® program director, **David Littell, JD, ChFC®, CFP®** *"the research is clearly showing that reverse mortgages, if used properly, can increase sustainability of retirement income and total wealth. It would be a disservice to financial advisors and their clients not to include this in our curriculum".*

Unfortunately, if a client mentions a reverse mortgage to the typical financial adviser, his questions are likely to be dismissed.

Beware: the more general and vague the reasons offered for not discussing a reverse mortgage, the more likely the adviser has not mastered either the changes in reverse mortgages, the studies supporting housing wealth inclusion in retirement plans, or both.

Clients may be intimidated when the adviser scoffs at a request for information on a reverse mortgage. Many advisers may dismiss the conversation by making statements like "you don't want one of those," "they are too expensive," "I can't talk to you about that or I will get in trouble," or the all-time misinformed but common mistake, "you don't want to give your house to the bank."

If an adviser states that the homeowner should wait to set up a HECM because he will receive more money when he is older, the adviser is giving incorrect advice for two reasons:

1. Although at any particular point in time, an older borrower is eligible for more money than a younger one, the credit allowed (Principal Limit) is much more sensitive to prevailing interest rates than to age.

Chart 14.1

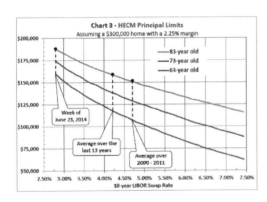

"Borrowers of different ages will be impacted by rising rates. If the 10-year swap rate goes up to its historic averages, benefits will be greatly reduced. Chart and explanation courtesy of Gerald Wagner, PhD, President of IBIS Software."

Rates won't stay low forever.

If the swap rate rises just 1.0% above its current level (from 2.71% to 3.71%), the money available to a 63-year-old will fall by 20%.

One can just let the new HECM lie fallow. Its line-of-credit capacity will grow each month, and when funds are finally accessed they are tax-free loan advances.

2. If the client waits until he is older to set up a HECM Line of Credit, he will have missed the compounding growth. (See **Chart 10.3**)

Why such resistance? Often advisers are unaware of what is changing because their initial training did not include housing wealth. Many advisers adhere to what they learned 20 or 30 years ago: If you go broke, *then* take out a reverse mortgage. It reflects a passive, "wait and see," attitude. It also reflects the emotional tie that many people have for "burning the mortgage" when they retire, and therefore being free of debt payments. It is an attitude that became ingrained long before reverse mortgages became available to the general public, and long before the general public had been switched from employer-provided defined benefit pensions to 401(k) accounts that retirees had to manage throughout retirement. They cling to this advice despite, as Dr. Sacks, Dr. Salter, Dr. Guttentag, and Dr. Pfau have demonstrated, relying on a reverse mortgage as a last resort results in the worst outcome. The notion that coordinating housing wealth in the plan may prevent portfolio exhaustion has not penetrated the financial planning community.

Some advisers will insist that FINRA, the self-regulatory entity policing broker-dealers, prohibits reverse mortgage lending. In fact, for some time, FINRA did recommend that reverse mortgages only be used as a "last resort." Dr. Sacks challenged FINRA by establishing that this is a mathematically incorrect statement. Ultimately FINRA did alter its language in October, 2013:

> *"FINRA is issuing this Alert to urge homeowners thinking about reverse mortgages to make informed decisions and carefully weigh all of their options before proceeding. And, if you do decide a reverse mortgage is right for you, be sure to make prudent use of your loan."[31]*

An adviser may refuse discussing housing wealth because his broker-dealer compliance officer forbids it. It is not clear why

---

31 *http://www.finra.org/investors/alerts/reverse-mortgages-avoiding-reversal-fortune*

compliance officers would want to avoid aiding clients in preserving portfolio value. Some certainly fear that rogue advisers would inappropriately encourage clients to tap home equity in order to sell the client more securities. Doing so may subject the retired client to greater risk since the securities could lose value.

What these broker-dealer compliance officers fail to understand is that current research does not suggest using housing wealth to purchase new securities, but rather advocates using housing wealth to protect against having to sell *existing* securities when their values are low.

The financial advising world is ill-equipped to evaluate housing in another crucial manner. Many advisers rely on financial planning software to prepare possible retirement plans for their clients. Unfortunately most software vendors do not provide asset projections that can evaluate a plan with and without incorporating housing wealth. The retiree who pays for a personalized, colorful financial plan produced by planner software, in effect, is getting only one side of the story. Without this information, the client cannot decide whether or not taking a reverse mortgage is suitable for his needs.

American retirees pay for advice, either through fees or commissions, or both. The cost is not insignificant. To place this cost in perspective, a client with a starting portfolio of $1,000,000 may pay his adviser a 1% "Assets Under Management" fee, or $10,000 the first year. That is $10,000 subtracted from the portfolio that will not be available to fund retirement years.[32]

To stay roughly on budget, this client could draw 4% of his portfolio the first year, or $40,000. The second year in retirement this client he would pay his adviser another 1% of remaining AUM. Advice comes at a cost, and advisers are obligated to provide varying standards of care.[33]

---

32 *A future value calculator at dinkytown.net values the loss of this $10,000 over a 30 year retirement at $57,444 at a 6% annual rate of return.*

33 *For a discussion about the differences between "fiduciary" versus "suitability "standards of advice, see http://www.investopedia.com/articles/ professionaleducation/11/suitability-fiduciary-standards.asp*

The point here is not that people do not benefit from financial planning advice, but that they are entitled to accurate information and *informed advice* about whether or not their housing wealth can aid cash flow survival. At the very least, an adviser who confers with his clients on the suitability of possibly including the housing wealth asset in a retirement plan provides more complete assistance than an adviser who refuses to discuss a reverse mortgage.

That some financial services firms reject learning how reverse mortgages work is even more perplexing when considering that AUM (Assets Under Management) is so important to fee generation, both at the retail level, and the mutual fund level. The Wall Street Journal reported in June 2015 that 401(k) withdrawals by Boomers exceeded contributions which will have an effect on large money managers. Dr. Sacks provides perspective:

> *"Suppose a retiree at age 65 has a portfolio worth $1 million. If that retiree decides to draw more than the SafeMax amount, and opts to use the Coordinated Strategy to manage his cash flow, clearly the mutual fund or other portfolio manager will retain more of the securities under management, for a longer time, than it would if the retiree were to use the Last Resort Strategy. As part of calculating cash flow survival, our program calculates how much remains in the portfolio at any time in the 30-year sequence; and it does so for both strategies. By simply applying an assumed 50 basis point annual fee (multiplying the amount in the portfolio), the program determines how much the portfolio manager earns from the portfolio. How much more is earned under the Coordinated Strategy than under the Last Resort Strategy? And when? Since the computer program uses Monte Carlo simulation, the results span a wide range. However, the mean of the difference between the mutual funds earnings over the 30-year period , under the Coordinated Strategy and the Last Resort Strategy, discounted to present value at a 5% discount rate, for the $1 million portfolio (with a home value of greater than*

$600,000) turns out to be about $50,000. Of course most of that difference occurs in the later years, but the 5% discount rate is quite conservative, and yields a result in "today's value" terms. Next, assume that, of the $1 trillion currently held in securities portfolios of people currently age 65 or older, 1/10 of 1% is held by people who own their homes and decide that they could benefit from using the Coordinated Strategy. That would represent $1 billion. If each $1 million in that $1 billion yields, on average, increased fees of $50,000, the overall gain to the portfolio manager(s) would be $50 million. Carrying that analysis into the future, as the rest of the baby-boomer generation comes into retirement, it seems reasonable to conclude that at least another $50 million of increased fees should be realized." Private Correspondence

Who Doesn't Need a Backup Plan For a Secure Retirement?[34]

Professionals thinking deeply about the challenges Baby Boomers face in funding their own retirements inevitably alight on housing wealth. Michael Kitces, MSFS, MTAX, CFP®, CLU, ChFC, RHU, REBC, CASL, has noted that a standard mortgage requiring repayment could be counter-productive if the goal is to improve cash flow. By having to make payments each month the client is deleveraging what he wanted to leverage in the first place. In comparison, a reverse mortgage leverages the housing asset to produce cash flow which may accomplish the client's goal more efficiently.

There simply is no way to know what the future holds. Establishing a well-priced emergency fund could be a wise strategy for just about anybody.

---

34 *http://mandelman.ml-implode.com/2014/01/who-doesnt-need-a-back-up-plan-for-a-secure-retirement/*

Summary

Sadly, many in the financial services community may know less about reverse mortgages than those who watch late night television. No doubt these omnipresent reverse mortgage infomercials have contributed to the product's bad reputation. Regardless, if your financial adviser is uninformed on the newly structured HECM and its costs, he should not dissuade you from having a conversation about a *possible* role the house can play in retirement. After all, you are paying for the advice.

CHAPTER 14

How Do I Choose an Ethical Lender and Get the Best Price?

As in any profession, there are scoundrels in reverse mortgage lending. It is important that the homeowner find a reputable lender. And few people realize that, once they engage with a lender, they can negotiate interest rates and closing costs just as they would do with any other mortgage.

If your adviser cannot recommend a dependable lending partner, it may take some work to find a competent lender. Unlike traditional mortgages, there are not banks and lenders for the HECM at every corner. The homeowner who lives outside metropolitan areas may have difficulty finding a lender with whom he can meet face to face.

Television ads, often featuring actors and ex-Senators, do provide options. The lenders who advertise in this manner are prompt in returning your call/email and will send out well-crafted DVDs and colorful, easy to understand materials.

Just like any mortgage, the client will be in driver's seat if he engages with two or three lenders. Some lenders will have more discretion on how they price loans than others. In general, if the lender is a Ginnie Mae[35] issuer, the company will stand to make money on future draws from the credit line known as "tails." These lenders, therefore, may be more willing to cut fees upfront since they are banking on participating in revenue during the full length of the loan. It certainly will not hurt to ask potential lending prospects if they securitize their loans through Ginnie Mae.

Brokers can discount heavily if pushed, particularly if they are caught up in a price war with another lender. Loan originators in broker shops, however, often are paid on the opening loan balance which could color their advice. Again, the borrower is best served in a reverse mortgage transaction by gathering bids from multiple sources.

All lenders can provide loan summary comparisons and amortization schedules demonstrating the interplay between upfront costs and home equity retention across varying interest rates. A homeowner would do well to keep in mind that the lender makes more money the higher the opening loan balance is. The profit from the secondary market on this initial "unpaid principal balance" can be quite high. This creates an incentive for lenders to originate loans with high initial draws, rather than starting with a larger line of credit.

If a lender is pushing for a high disbursement at closing, this a red flag that he may be thinking about his commission rather than your best interest. Even worse, some lenders suggest that the client take a large disbursement at closing, and then pay down the loan in the future. Again, this suggestion is a red flag that the lender is trying to maximize his own revenue.

Although the HECM formula for credit limits are set by the FHA via the Principal Limit factors, the amount of money that the client starts with is affected by interest rate margins and fees. The good news is that you can negotiate these elements. When

---

35 The **Government National Mortgage Association (GNMA)**, *or* **Ginnie Mae**. *A government corporation within the Department of Housing and Urban Development (HUD), Ginnie Mae's mission is to expand affordable housing. The Ginnie Mae guarantee allows mortgage lenders to obtain a better price for their loans in the capital markets. Lenders then can use the proceeds to make new mortgage loans available to consumers.*

applying for a traditional mortgage, clients fare better if they get lenders competing for their business. The same thing is true with reverse mortgages. What the homeowner negotiates will depend on how he is planning to use the HECM.

If the HECM will be in place for a Short Period of Time

This client would want to choose a HECM with the lowest possible closing costs, and no origination fee. Closing costs can be "bought down" by taking a higher interest rate. Just like traditional mortgages, over-par, "Premium Pricing," can be used to fund lender credits to reduce closing cost. The client can calculate how long it will take the loan balance growing at a higher rate to catch up to the reduction in upfront fees.

A client may choose this strategy in order to start an encore profession. The HECM can be paid down, or retired completely, without penalty when the business starts making money. Should he elect to keep the HECM in place, the Line of Credit (just a $50 loan balance needed) would grow at an accelerated rate due to the higher interest rate.

If the HECM will be used to Establish a Standby Line of Credit

This client may benefit from taking a higher interest rate to buy down closing costs and lender fees. Since he is planning on setting up his Line of Credit as a standby fund, his loan balance will be low and accruing at a slow pace. The higher interest rate, however, will generate higher growth in the Line of Credit.

If the HECM is used to Purchase a New Principal Residence

Most clients who choose to purchase a new home using the HECM select the highest possible initial credit limit. Since what they provide as their down payment is the difference between the home value and the lump sum HECM payout, they are often overly focused on the down payment, rather than the overall cost of the loan. These borrowers can benefit from negotiating with different lenders to strike the right balance between upfront fees, interest rates, and lump sum disbursements, and their own resulting down payment. Because their initial loan balance will be high and quite profitable to the lender, they are in a powerful negotiating position. Homebuyers should evaluate whether or not it makes sense to provide a higher down payment in order to take advantage of the .5% versus 2.5% MIP.

If the HECM will be used to Refinance an Existing Traditional Mortgage/HELOC

The lump sum disbursals on these loans are usually high. Your negotiating leverage is powerful since the lender profit is substantial at the loan's outset. Again, don't be afraid to engage two or more lenders to bid for the business. If asked, the lenders will provide loan summaries and amortization schedules demonstrating the interplay between upfront costs and home equity retention based on various interest rates.

If the HECM will be disbursed in a Term or Tenure Payment Schedule

The homeowner taking a Term or Tenure Payment will not have quite the same leverage as a full draw, lump sum client. Yet it is still possible to negotiate terms. Competing lenders will provide loan summaries and amortization schedules for comparison, if requested.

Negotiating Interest Rates and Fees

The client will need to choose between taking a fixed-rate reverse mortgage, or an adjustable rate. The drawback to fixed-rate loans is that they do not provide for a line of credit. Even if the loan is paid down substantially, it is considered a close-ended loan and no future draws may be taken. The Mortgage Professor expands on the differences between taking a fixed-rate traditional mortgage and a fixed-rate reverse mortgage:

"The reasons for selecting an adjustable rather than a fixed rate are also different. On a standard mortgage, few borrowers opt for an adjustable-rate because of fears that they will still have their mortgage when the initial rate period ends, and that a rate increase at that time will increase their required payment. Many seniors considering a reverse mortgage bring along a negative mindset from their experience with (or what they have heard about) adjustable rates on standard mortgages. Some begin the process by expressing a strong preference for a fixed-rate reverse mortgage, which may or may not meet their needs.

The rationale for preferring fixed rates on standard mortgages, which is to avoid the risk of a payment increase, has no applicability to reverse mortgages, which have no required payment. The benefit of the fixed rate on a reverse mortgage is only that the borrower knows in advance exactly how fast the debt secured by his home will grow. The downside is that the fixed-rate HECM offers only one way to draw funds, which is to take a lump sum at closing.

The fixed rate HECM reverse mortgage is primarily for seniors who plan to use all or most of their borrowing power right away. Their intent is to pay off an existing mortgage, buy a house, purchase a single-premium annuity, or transact for some other purpose that requires a large and immediate payment. The fixed-rate HECM does not allow the borrower to reserve any borrowing power for future use. Once it is closed, no more funds can be drawn."[36]

In contrast to the fixed-rate, full draw option, the Adjustable Rate HECM performs like a revolving line of credit. Payments may have been made against the loan balance. That payment is immediately available in the line of credit.

---

36 *http://www.mtgprofessor.com/A%20-20Reverse%20Mortgages/adjustable_rate_versus_fixed_rate.html*

There are <u>three</u> different interest rates used in the Adjustable Rate HECM:

a. Note Rate

b. Effective Rate

c. Expected Rate

Note Rate: Adjustable Rate HECMs are configured with monthly adjusting or annually adjusting interest rates. The beginning interest rate is known as the **Initial Rate**. This rate will adjust monthly or yearly. The new note rate will determine how much interest is accruing on the money borrowed. The monthly adjustable rate has an interest rate cap of 10%. The yearly adjustable cap is 5%.

The Adjustable HECM is based today on the one-month Libor. This rate is known as the **Index**. The lender adds a **Margin** of roughly 2.25 to 4.00 %. This margin can be negotiated during the application period. Higher margins are known as Premium Pricing and can be used to fund lender credits against closing costs.

The adjustable index rate will fluctuate with the market over the course of the loan. Once the loan is in place the margin cannot be altered by either the lender or borrower. Both the index source (usually the one-month Libor) and margin are locked in and can only be changed through a refinance transaction.

Effective Rate: The actual rate at which the loan balance is accruing interest and MIP charges. The cost of the loan is increased by Mortgage Insurance Premiums (MIP) assessed by FHA. In effect, adding the MIP creates an "effective interest rate" higher than the interest rate alone. Today the ongoing MIP rate is 1.25% annually. For example, if a client has chosen a margin of 2.0 and the one-month Libor is at .175 in any given month, his Note Rate is 1/12 of 2.175= .181. The actual Effective Rate will include 1/12 of the annual MIP of 1.25 =.104. Therefore, the loan balance, that month will incur an Effective Interest Rate of .285.

Note Rate	One-month LIBOR	Varies month to month	0.20%
	Lender's margin	Fixed for each loan	+ 2.25% to 4.00%
Mortgage Insurance Premium (MIP)	Set by FHA	Fixed for all loans	+ 1.25%
Effective Interest Rate (Compounding)			= 3.70% to 5.45%

Expected Average Rate : It is important to understand the implications of choosing a particular margin. The margin will affect the accumulation of interest on money borrowed,which will deplete equity. In addition, the margin selected for accumulating interest will be the same for the credit determinant rate (Expected Rate) as it is for the accrual rate (Initial Rate) on the loan balance. The rate used to determine initial available credit is termed the "**Expected Average Rate**." This rate is meant to be a predictor of the rates that will be charged over the life of the loan. Whereas the accrual rate index on monthly adjusting loans is the one-month Libor, the "Expected Rate" uses the 10-year LIBOR swap rate as its index. The 10-year Libor swap rate is available from the Federal Reserve.[37] *Choosing a higher margin can reduce the initial available credit.* There is, in addition, a floor below which additional credit will not be possible.

Expected Interest Rate Determines Available Funds Calculates Term/ Tenure	10-year LIBOR Swap	Set at Closing	2.11%
	Lender's margin	Same Margin as Initial Rate Chosen By Borrower	+ 2.25% to 4.00%

Once the loan is in place, the loan balance will compound at the "effective interest" rate. As shown above, the effective interest rate is the sum of the monthly applicable interest rate (note rate) plus the 1/12 annual MIP of 1.25%.

---

37 *http://www.federalreserve.gov/releases/h15/update/*

Clients may choose a higher interest rate to buy down upfront fees. This could be desirable if the client intends to maintain a low loan balance and is primarily interested in maximizing growth in the HECM Line of Credit.

FHA Counseling is Mandatory Before Application: How to Find a Counselor

There is an important consumer safeguard to protect borrowers from mistakenly concluding that, since there are no payments, the reverse mortgage is something other than debt. Potential borrowers must complete a counseling session before making an application with a lender. Counselors review the loan obligations, and emphasize that taxes and insurance are the responsibility of the borrower. Likewise, the counselors explain that the loan is accumulating interest and FHA mortgage insurance premiums, which will need to be paid back when the last participant dies, moves, or sells.[38]

Finding a Lender

The National Reverse Mortgage Lenders Association maintains a lender search tool. Use the search tool to locate lenders by state (specifically the state in which the property is located). All lenders are members of the National Reverse Mortgage Lenders Association, licensed to originate reverse mortgages in the states in which they are listed, and have signed NRMLA's Code of Conduct & Professional Responsibility. [39]

Filing a Complaint

Complaints may be submitted to the Consumer Protection Financial Bureau at http://www.consumerfinance.gov/complaint.
Phone: (855) 411-CFPB (2372)
TTY/TDD (855) 729-CFPB (2372)

---

38 *HUD-approved counselors can be found at http://www.hud.gov/offices/hsg/sfh/hcc/hcs.cfm*

39 *http://www.reversemortgage.org/FindaLender.aspx*

For Those Who Have a Reverse Mortgage Now

Regulations have changed on how someone living in the house, but not on the loan documents, will be treated once the primary borrower leaves the house permanently. The CFPB recommends:

Here are 3 things you or your loved ones should do if you have a reverse mortgage:

1. Verify who is on the loan. If you took out a reverse mortgage with two borrowers, check with your reverse mortgage to make sure its loan records are accurate. Call your servicer to find out what names are listed on your loan. They may be able to help you over the phone. See your reverse mortgage statement for the phone number, and ask them to send you this information in writing for your records. You can also write a letter requesting information.

2. If your reverse mortgage is in the name of only one spouse, make a plan for the non-borrowing spouse. If your reverse mortgage is in the name of only one spouse, contact your loan servicer to find out if the non-borrowing spouse may qualify for a repayment deferral. A repayment deferral allows a non-borrowing spouse to remain living in the home after the death of the borrowing spouse. If not, make a plan in the event the borrowing spouse dies first and the loan becomes due. If you or your spouse are not on the loan but believe that you should be, promptly seek legal advice. If you have enough remaining equity in your home, you could consider taking out a new reverse mortgage with both spouses. You'll have to pay loan fees again, however, for the new loan. If the non-borrowing spouse can't pay off the reverse mortgage when the borrowing spouse passes away, he or she might consider a new traditional mortgage if they have the income and credit to qualify. Also consider other family members that would be willing to cosign on such a loan. Some surviving spouses may need to sell the home and make plans for where they will live after the home is sold. Contact a HUD approved counselor to discuss options.

3. Talk to your children and heirs-make a plan for any non-borrowing members living in the house. [40]

---

40 *http://www.consumerfinance.gov/blog/consumer-advisory-three-steps-you-should-take-if-you-have-a-reverse-mortgage/*

Summary: Other Red Flags

The CFPB reports that mortgages of all kinds generate the highest number of complaints to that agency. Complaints on reverse mortgages are relatively rare. From December 1, 2011 through December 31, 2014, CFPB handled approximately 1,200 reverse mortgage complaints. Reverse mortgage complaints comprise about 1% of all mortgage complaints, regardless of age, submitted to the CFPB. Consumers' most frequent complaints involve their inability to make certain changes to the loans, as well as loan servicing difficulties.[41] Although servicers do provide monthly statements, they are opaque in the extreme. And unfortunately those answering the phone are often poorly trained and cannot explain most of what is printed on the statement.

Like the traditional mortgage world, there are behaviors that could indicate that your best interests are not being considered. Any lender that pushes you to make a rash decision cannot be trusted. If requested by the homeowner, ethical lenders are only too happy to meet with the adult children, financial adviser, CPA, banker, or others to help improve comprehension on how the HECM works. Lenders that encourage taking out larger lump sums than needed likely are focusing on their commissions. Lenders that decline to provide a variety of loan summary comparisons and accompanying amortization schedules for both adjustable-rate and fixed- rate options with a full range of interest rate choices are not serving your best interest. Lenders that push for fixed- rate, full draw loans may be motivated by the profit on the sale of the note on the secondary market.

Some lenders are agnostic in the way they compensate their loan officers. This means that regardless of how the money is disbursed, the loan officer is paid at a set rate. Other lenders incent their loan officers based on the initial draw taken at closing. You certainly are entitled to ask how commissions are computed.

---

41 *http://files.consumerfinance.gov/f/201502_cfpb_report_snapshot-reverse-mortgage-complaints-december-2011-2014.pdf*

If a loan officer states that the HECM Line of Credit is "earning interest," he is either being deceptive or does not understand that the amount available to be borrowed from the HECM LOC increases over time . The HECM LOC increase is just an opportunity to borrow more against home equity. The amount of increase is dependent upon the interest rate, as described earlier, but no interest is earned by the borrower on a Line of Credit.

On rare occasions, some financial planners have colluded with lenders to use a client's home equity inappropriately. You should be wary of any third party who is linking any mortgage, reverse mortgages included, to other financial products. Housing wealth may not be used to buy securities. Securities can lose value and the client would have lost home equity by embarking on a mortgage, a reverse mortgage included. This situation would be a double whammy and is not permissible.

CHAPTER 15

What's the Application Process?

Once the client has obtained a counseling certificate, and has chosen a lender, an application is taken by a loan officer, either in person or on the phone. Commonly, the applicant provides an appraisal fee (less than $500) at application. The interest rate that applies to determining credit (Expected Rate) will be frozen for a short period of time. At closing, whichever rate provides the highest Principal Limit, either the current rate Expected Rate, or the Expected Rate at application, will be used. The initial accrual interest rate will be tied to that week's one-month Libor, if a montly adjustable rate HECM.

An FHA- approved appraiser will schedule a visit to assess the home, both inside and out. Over the next few weeks, the homeowner will be asked to provide documents illustrating his financial situation. Gathering as many of these documents as possible before application can reduce stress during the process. Anyone who has taken out a traditional home loan knows how irritating the escalating requests for documents can be, not to mention being asked two or three times for the same information. Needless to say, the client should keep a copy of every document sent to the mortgage company.

Should the appraisal come back lower than expected, the homeowner can appeal. Sometimes properties themselves are ineligible for FHA lending. Competent loan officers are adept at avoiding these mistakes. It is against the law, however, for a lender to refuse to take an application for credit if the borrower so wishes.

Since April, 2015, applicants are required to undergo a financial assessment. The financial assessment will determine whether or not a potential borrower meets willingness and capacity qualifiers. If the applicant's past credit history does not demonstrate willingness to meet his homeowner obligations, HECM regulations require that that a portion of his proceeds be placed in a **Fully Funded Life Expectancy Set-Aside (LESA).** This set-aside is based on life expectancy and the total predicted tax and insurance payments for the future. It is possible that the LESA could be so high the borrower will not qualify for the HECM. For others, this set aside is a relief. They are happy to have someone else make sure that their taxes and insurance payments are made.

If the applicant can demonstrate willingness, but does not meet residual income guidelines, HECM guidelines require a **Partially Funded Set-Aside**. The partial funding is for applicants who meet the credit requirements of willingness but may struggle to havingenough cash flow to make their tax and insurance payments. This Set-Aside, which can be much smaller, is used to draw funds from the HECM twice a year. The lender sends the funds to the borrower who is responsible for satisfying his own tax and insurance obligations.

Once you have been approved, a lawyer's office or title company will complete a title search and issue title insurance. Homeowner's insurance is required. Flood insurance may be as well. All of these closing costs, including various state and local taxes, will be assessed along with upcoming property taxes. These borrower costs will be deducted from available funds, unless you decide to pay them upfront. These fees, if not paid up front, become part of the beginning loan balance.

Just like you would for any mortgage closing, you should insist on studying the HUD-1 closing document before attending the closing. The last thing you want to do is see the numbers for the first time under the pressure of sitting in an unfamiliar office with countless papers to sign. Fortunately loans that are considered a re-finance, (not purchase loans), require a 3-day Right of Rescission. If you have requested a disbursal at closing, those funds will be made available at the end of the rescission period. In a few weeks, the loan servicer will be in touch with you in order to arrange for scheduled payments, and/or Line of Credit draws.

The lender may or may not "service" the loan. This is a standard practice in mortgage lending.[42] The client can expect his servicing to change hands. It is important to watch for notices advising the that this relationship has changed. Notices are required by law to precede a change.

The servicer will send the homeowner monthly statements indicating loan balance, interest rate changes, draws, available Line of Credit, and voluntary payments received. The statements will include servicer contact information.

---

42 *For a discussion of the difference between a servicer and your lender, see http://www.consumerfinance.gov/askcfpb/198/whats-the-difference-between-a-mortgage-lender-and-a-servicer.html*

CHAPTER 16

Typical FAQs

Who Qualifies and What Properties are Eligible?

The mortgage company will provide the potential borrower with a copy of *Use Your Home to Stay at Home* published by the National Council on Aging. [43]

What follows is a typical summation of homeowner qualifications, property eligibility and other basic components of FHA HECM lending provided by lenders and NRMLA:

What if one person is 62 and the other is 68?

The age of the youngest person is used.

Does my credit matter and will a credit report be required?

Yes, a credit report will be required. The lender is looking for federal liens and evidence that property obligations have been met in the past. Any federal lien would need to be satisfied before the HECM could be used. Credit scores don't matter but payment history is analyzed.

What if I have a bankruptcy or tax lien on my credit report?

Unlike a traditional mortgage, a HECM is not provided based on credit scores alone. A Chapter 7 Bankruptcy appearing on your credit report will need to have been discharged prior to closing. A

---

43 *For a downloadable copy :http://www.ncoa.org/news-ncoa-publications/ publications/ncoa_reverse_mortgage_booklet_073109.pdf*

Chapter 13 Bankruptcy appearing on your credit report must show a satisfactory payment history and may possibly have to be paid through closing. You may also need to provide a letter of explanation for these matters.

Is the rate fixed or variable?

You can choose fixed or variable. However, a fixed rate can be chosen only where the entire amount of initial available credit is drawn at the outset. This results in a high balance and does not allow for a revolving credit line.

What is the HECM Counseling Certificate?

FHA requires each applicant to complete a counseling session with an independent third-party counselor over the phone. The counselor will ask you questions and answer any questions you have to confirm your understanding of the HECM program. After this session a Counseling Certificate will be issued showing completion.

What are the closing costs?

The closing costs are similar to those of a regular FHA mortgage. There is a Mortgage Insurance Premium (MIP) that is based on the appraised value of the home. There are also third party fees like title, appraisal, and recording.

Who owns title to the home?

The borrower is fully vested on the title of the home. You can never lose title to your home, so long as taxes, insurance, and any homeowner association dues are kept current. Additionally, the home must remain in good condition and serve as your primary residence.

What if I decide to sell my house in 10 years and the house has depreciated and I owe more than what I can sell it for?

It's not your problem, the house will be sold for fair market value and the proceeds will pay off the mortgage. Any deficit will be paid by FHA to the lender.

Isn't the HECM just another program that will end up getting the Federal Government in trouble?

No, this is not a taxpayer-funded program. Every person who acquires an FHA insured loan contributes to the FHA mortgage insurance fund. In the case of regular (non-HECM) FHA mortgage insured loans, the borrower has part of his monthly payment go toward the FHA mortgage insurance fund. In the case of the HECM program, the lender pays FHA 1.25% of the loan balance per year (which in turn accrues on the loan balance) which creates a continuous stream of dollars to the insurance fund.

What happens when both spouses die?

The house will be left to the estate and will be settled the exact same way as any other estate with a house involved. An appraised value will be determined and the house will be sold for fair market value. If the sale price exceeds the mortgage balance then the difference will go to the estate. If the sale price is less than the mortgage balance, the estate will NOT be responsible for that deficit.

Isn't this program only for people who don't have money?

The program is being used by middle income earners as well as millionaires. It allows financially savvy people to use the value of their home as an additional source of retirement assets instead of leaving it tied up, illiquid and unavailable, while still fully retaining the shelter and enjoyment of the home.

How does the bank/lender make its money?

On a traditional mortgage the bank receives interest as part of the monthly payment. The HECM interest is accruing in the background which causes the balance to grow over time. The bank or investor makes money on the total interest accrued at the time the house is sold.

What property types are excluded?

Currently Co-Ops are excluded. A HECM may not attach to a vacation home or investment property. Condos are permitted if a

FHA condo approval can be obtained. Multi-family homes may be eligible if the borrower lives there.

Is there a limit on the amount of funds you can access during the initial year?

If you are eligible for a $100,000 loan, for example, you can take $60,000, or 60 % of that sum. There are exceptions. You can withdraw a bit more if you have an existing mortgage, or other liens on the property, that exceed the 60 % limit. You must pay off these "mandatory obligations" as the FHA terms them, and this is usually done with the proceeds from the HECM. You can withdraw enough to pay off these obligations, plus another 10 % of the maximum allowable amount—in which case that's an extra $10,000, or 10 % of $100,000. You are permitted to exceed the 60% limit if you are using the HECM to purchase a new principal residence. Loan proceeds can be taken as a lump sum, as a line of credit or as fixed monthly payments, either for a fixed amount of time or for as long as you remain in the home. You can also combine these options, for example, taking part of the proceeds as a lump sum and leaving the balance in a line of credit. Fees can be paid out of the loan proceeds. This means you incur very little out-of-pocket expense to get a reverse mortgage. Your only out-of-pocket expense is the appraisal fee and maybe a charge for counseling depending on the counseling organization you work with. Together, these two fees will total a few hundred dollars. Very low-income homeowners are exempted from being charged for counseling. When you ultimately pay off the loan, the final balance equals the amount of funds borrowed, plus annual mortgage insurance premiums, servicing fees and interest. The loan balance grows while you are living in the home. In other words, when you sell or leave the house, you owe more than you originally borrowed. Look at it this way: A traditional mortgage is a balloon full of air that gets smaller each time you make a payment. A reverse mortgage is an empty balloon that grows larger as time passes. With a Home Equity Conversion Mortgage or HECM, no matter how large the loan balance, you never have to pay more than the appraised value of the home or the sale price. This feature is referred to as "non-recourse." If the loan balance exceeds the appraised value of the home, then the FHA insurance fund absorbs that loss. You are responsible for paying property taxes, homeowners insurance, condo fees and other financial charges. Any lapse in these policies can trigger a default on your loan. To help reduce future defaults, the FHA requires lenders to conduct a financial assessment of all prospective borrowers. Lenders will analyze all income sources—including pensions, Social Security, IRAs and 401(k) plans—as well as your credit history. They will look closely at how much money is left over after paying typical living expenses. If a lender determines that you have sufficient income left over, then you won't have to worry about having any funds set aside to pay for future tax and insurance payments. If, however, a lender determines that you may not be able to keep up with property taxes and insurance payments, they will be authorized to set aside a certain amount of funds from your loan to pay future charges. [44]

44 *http://www.reversemortgage.org/About/FeaturesofReverseMortgages.aspx*

CHAPTER 17

What's the Cost of Delaying?

The HECM reverse mortgage has evolved to meet the needs of mainstream America. The original intent of the program was to help retirees liquidate home wealth throughout retirement, as needed. But when equity consumption ran off the rails in the housing bubble, the program, and individuals ill-suited for reverse mortgages, suffered. In response, the FHA has restructured the program to encourage using it in a conservative and prudent fashion.

Whether or not an individual homeowner elects to consume his housing wealth is a decision best made with facts and thoughtful analysis, not emotions and half-baked preconceptions. It could be a costly mistake to ignore the protections a reverse mortgage can provide, particularly over a 30-40 year retirement.

Peter Neuwirth, FSA, describes how Present Value considerations assist us in making decisions today while keeping in mind what may happen in the future. [45] Yet many people just avoid making financial decisions altogether. If you choose not think about it ,the cost to you in the future of not having established at least a LOC on your house could be high. The randomness of what the future holds may help you decide whether or not your personal approach to retirement planning will include using your home.

---

45 *Neuwirth, Peter. What's Your Future Worth: Using Present Value to Make Better Decisions*

There are some very good reasons to not wait until you *need* one to apply for a reverse mortgage:

1. If you wait for portfolio ruin, your financial situation may have deteriorated to such a degree, that, under new financial assessment rules, you will not be able to qualify.[46]

2. If you do not set up a HECM Line of Credit early in retirement, you lose the compounding growth of a liquid asset.

3. If you do not set up a HECM Line of Credit early in retirement, it cannot serve as an alternate source of income should you encounter a dangerous early sequence of bad investment returns.

4. Because interest rates are low today, the initial credit limit is high. If you wait until you need a reverse mortgage, rates may be significantly higher, and consequently your your credit limit could be substantially lower. This could prevent you from replacing a traditional mortgage (with monthly payments) with a HECM just when you need it most.

5. Since your house is an undiversified asset, placing a guaranteed, growing Line of Credit on it allows you to hedge against declining housing values.

The Ultimate Interest Only Mortgage

So, for the reader, I offer what I would do early in retirement with my own home. I would open a HECM Line of Credit with a minimum balance of $50. I would accomplish this by choosing a higher interest rate margin. By taking a higher rate, I would be able to negotiate with my lender to avoid incurring closing costs. The ongoing interest and MIP costs for this $50 balance would be next to nothing. I would just let the LOC grow and not use the available funds unless a clear need arose. Thus my reverse mortgage is functioning as a *Standby Emergency Fund*.

---

46 *Thank you to Mark Schumacher for this observation.* Private Correspondence.

Now here is what is important to me. If I did need to draw substantial funds from the HECM, say to avoid drawing on my portfolio at a loss, I would treat the HECM as if it were an interest only (I-O) loan. This means that I would make voluntary payments on the accruing interest and MIP to keep the loan balance low, and the compounding interest under control. In other words, I would have the use of the amount borrowed, tax-free, but would avoid the compounding that can accumulate so quickly with a reverse mortgage.

Only a reverse mortgage allows this flexibility. By setting up a HECM, there is no commitment to any particular loan amount, or a proscribed repayment schedule. It is my choice how to use the money, how to allow interest to accrue, or not, and how to pay the loan back.

So you can see that my plan is conservative. Keeping the loan balance low would give me the most flexibility if I wanted to move later in retirement and needed equity from my home to make the move. If I lived very long in my house, however, and I could not make the interest payments comfortably, I would change my strategy and start letting the interest accrue. In other words, if bad stuff happened, I would fall back on the non-recourse guarantee that the house, not me, would pay the loan back. So I have converted the risk for falling property values and my own longevity to the FHA Mortgage Insurance pool, not me or my estate. I would be at peace with this outcome, because like every other HECM customer, I contributed to the mortgage insurance fund for this very protection.

So for better or worse, after years in the industry, this is the scenario that I have decided would work for me. Everyone is different, and encumbering the home with debt is never a decision to be made rashly. Yet above all, it is a decision deserving to be made with facts, not fabrications.

Perhaps you note a bit of a bit of fanaticism on my part? Without getting overwrought, I admit that I am on a mission to inform American retirees, and those they trust for financial advice, on how a reverse mortgage really works, how much it really costs, and how it can help other assets.

I thank you, the reader, for opening your mind to what must have seemed an unlikely topic. I hope that you agree now that yes, a reverse mortgage isn't for everybody but it isn't wrong for anybody, either. [47]

47 David W. Johnson, Ph.D., is an associate professor of finance at the University of Wisconsin. http://mandelman.ml-implode.com/2014/09/university-professors-research-reverse-mortgages-set-record-straight-a-mandelman-matters-podcast/

CHAPTER 18

Resources

4235.1 HUD HECM HANDBOOK

http://portal.hud.gov/hudportal/HUD?src=/program_offices/administration/hudclips/handbooks/hsgh/4235.1

HUD/FHA Mortgagee Letters

http://portal.hud.gov/hudportal/HUD?src=/program_offices/administration/hudclips/letters/mortgagee

Mortgagee Letters

Previous years:					
	2014	2009	1999	1989	1979
	2013	2008	1998	1988	1978
	2012	2007	1997	1987	1976
	2011	2006	1996	1986	
	2010	2005	1995	1985	
		2004	1994	1984	
		2003	1993	1983	
		2002	1992	1982	
		2001	1991	1981	
		2000	1990	1980	

Document Number	Title
15-09	Home Equity Conversion Mortgage (HECM) Program – Life Expectancy Set-Aside Growth Rate and Clarification to Section 3.98 of the HECM Financial Assessment and Property Charge Guide
15-08	Electronic Appraisal Delivery (EAD) portal for Federal Housing Administration (FHA) Insured Single Family Mortgages
15-07	Trial Payment Plans Associated with HUD's Loss Mitigation Loan Modification Options for Forward Mortgages
15-06	Home Equity Conversion Mortgage (HECM) - Delay in Effective Date for Financial Assessment and Property Charge Funding Requirements for the Payment of Certain Property Charges
15-05	Notice of Program Eligibility for HUD Insured Housing Programs for All People Regardless of Sexual Orientation, Gender Identity or Marital Status as Required by HUD's Equal Access Rule
15-04	Revised Notification to Homeowners of Availability of Housing Counseling Services
15-03	Mortgagee Optional Election Assignment for Home Equity Conversion Mortgages (HECMs) with FHA Case Numbers assigned prior to August 4, 2014
15-02	Home Equity Conversion Mortgage (HECM) Program: Policy Guidance and Certifications for Eligible and Ineligible Non-Borrowing HECM Spouses and Seasoning Requirements Guidance
15-01	Reduction of Federal Housing Administration (FHA) annual Mortgage Insurance Premium (MIP) rates and Temporary Case Cancellation Authority

Account Duration Patent (Barry H. Sacks, PhD, JD)
http://accountdurationpatent.com/

Agencies on Aging
http://www.n4a.org/

Aging in Place Institute
http://www.louistenenbaum.com/

American College of Financial Services Retirement Income Certified Professional
https://ricp.theamericancollege.edu/

American Society of Aging
http://www.asaging.org/

Boston College Center for Retirement Research
Using Home Equity in Retirement Downloadable
http://crr.bc.edu/booklets-brochures/

Blue Ocean Global Wealth
https://www.blueoceanglobalwealth.com/

Calculator for Determining HECM Funds Available
www.newretirement.com

Certified Financial Planners
http://www.plannersearch.org/Pages/Home.aspx

Consumer Financial Protection Bureau
http://www.consumerfinance.gov/

Eldercare Locator
www.eldercare.gov or 1-800-677-1116 is a source of information about the regional Area Agencies on Aging and local aging service providers that can help with information about additonal benefits.

FINRA Broker Check
http://brokercheck.finra.org/

Financial Calculators
http://dinkytown.com/

Funding Longevity Task Force
The mission of this Task Force is to develop and advance, for Boomers and their financial advisors, a rational and objective understanding of the role that housing wealth can play in prudent planning for retirement income. *www.fltaskforce.org*

Gerontology Consulting/Aging and Business Strategies
sandratimmermann1@gmail.com

HECM Counselor Study Guide
http://www.hecmcounselors.org/prospective-hecm-counselors/study-materials

HECM for Purchase Calculator
*http://rmc.ibisreverse.com/rmc_pages/rmc_hfhp/rmc_hfhp_1.**aspx***

HECM Retirement Calculators
http://www.financinglongevity.com/calculators.html

National Association of Elder Lawyers
https://www.naela.org/

National Association of Insurance and Financial Advisors
http://www.naifa.org/about-naifa

National Association of Personal Financial Advisors
http://napfa.org/

Michael E. Kitces MSFS, MTAX, CFP˚, CLU, ChFC, RHU, REBC, CASL
https://www.kitces.com/

Licensing for Financial Professionals
www.professionalmortgagealliance.com

National Association of Home Builders Aging in Place Certification

http://www.nahb.org/category.aspx?sectionID=686

National Council on Aging
http://www.ncoa.org/

NCOA Booklet *Use Your Home to Stay at Home* **Downloadable**
http://www.ncoa.org/enhance-economic-security/home-equity/
https://www.linkedin.com/pub/barbara-stucki/6/548/471

National Institute of Health *Making Your Web site Senior Friendly*
http://www.nlm.nih.gov/pubs/checklist.pdf

NRMLA Lendor Directory
http://www.reversemortgage.org/FindaLender.aspx

NRMLA HECM Calculator
http://www.reversemortgage.org/About/ReverseMortgageCalculator.aspx

NRMLA Guide for Finding a Counselor
http://www.reversemortgage.org/YourRoadmap/3Counseling.aspx

Retirement Income Industry Association (RIIA)
http://riia-usa.org/

Senior Real Estate Specialists (Realtors)
http://www.seniorsrealestate.com/

Silver Slippers Fitness
https://www.silversneakers.com/about/faq

Social Security Detailed Benefit Calculator
http://socialsecurity.gov/OACT/anypia/anypia.html

Social Security Optimization by Mary Beth Franklin (Ebook)
http://www.investmentnews.com/section/retirement2

Social Security Consulting Services
http://czarnowskiconsulting.com/about.html

Stephanie Moulton, PhD, John Glenn School of Public Affairs

http://glennschool.osu.edu/faculty/moulton.html

Texas Tech University School of Personal Financial Planning
http://www.depts.ttu.edu/pfp/

Think Reverse by Atare Agbamu
http://www.thinkreverse.com/

The Mortgage Professor
http://www.mtgprofessor.com/

Thomas C. B. Davison, MA, PhD, CFP®
http://toolsforretirementplanning.com/

Technology
http://www.ageinplacetech.com/

Transportation
http://www.seniortransportation.net/Partners.aspx

Wade Pfau, PhD, CFA, Professor of Retirement Income The American College
http://retirementresearcher.com

Women's Institute for a Secure Retirement
http://www.wiserwomen.org/

3 in 4 Need More *Long Term Care Planning Essentials* Downloadable
http://www.3in4needmore.com/wp-content/uploads/2013/02/3in4-Essentials-Book.pdf

55+ Communities
http://activeadultliving.com

CHAPTER 19

Glossary

Adjustable Rate HECM An option selected by homeowner. The index rate can change either monthly or annually. HECM adjustable-rate loans can be indexed to either the Treasury (CMT) rate or the London Interbank Offered Rate (LIBOR). A given loan must use either Treasury or LIBOR for both the Initial and the Expected Rates. Some lenders offer a monthly adjusting HECM with a 5% lifetime cap increase. The annually adjusting HECM uses the one-year LIBOR rate as its index. It generally has a 2% cap on annual changes and a 5% lifetime cap.

Amortization The process of paying off debt with payments allotted to carrying costs (interest), and principal.

Annuitize A right to receive periodic payments, usually fixed in size, for life or a term of years that is created by a contract or other legal document. The HECM Tenure Payment Option "annuitizes" a portion of the house.

Bankruptcy Lender shall have no obligation to make further Loan Advances on or following the date that a petition for bankruptcy of borrower is filed. At application Chapter 7 or Chapter 11 Bankruptcies must be discharged or dismissed. If the credit report says that the bankruptcy was dismissed or discharged over a year ago, no additional documents are required. If it was dismissed or discharged less than a year ago or if the credit report does not show a dismissal, a court order signed by the judge or a credit supplement evidencing the discharge/dismissal may be submitted as proof of the discharge or dismissal. Chapter 13 may pay the bankruptcy off at the closing or continue with the bankruptcy and the reverse mortgage. The Borrower still has to pay off any liens against the property, and any federal debt. The borrower will need permission from the court to do so.

Cap An upper limit on the interest rate that applies to a loan, e.g. an adjustable rate mortgage.

Combination Payment Option Selecting one or more payment options to be used simultaneously.

Co-ops Cooperatives were authorized by Congress in 2008, but the implementing regulations have not been issued. Therefore, a HECM cannot be placed on a cooperative property at present.

Day 366 The day when access to remaining Line of Credit is allowed at .5% initial MIP.

Delinquent Federal Debt Outstanding Federal debt is acceptable if the borrower has a payment agreement and is making payments as agreed.

Effective Rate The interest assessed on HECM loan balance that includes Mortgage Insurance Premium.

Eligible Non-Borrowing Spouse A spouse, declared at closing, who will be eligible for a deferral period should the borrower leave the home permanently. Refer to most recent Mortgagee Letters for NBS treatment for loans originated before August 4, 2014.

Expected Average Rate HECM Credit Determinant Rate. The Expected Rate is fixed for the life of the loan and is used for any future payment plan change calculations. Currently the Expected Rate is the 10-year LIBOR swap rate. http://www.federalreserve.gov/releases/h15/update/. It is never used to calculate accrued interest once the loan has closed. Rather, this rate is meant to be a predictor of the rates that could be charged over the life of the loan. The higher the Expected Rate, the less money is available at closing. For the purposes of calculating the Principal Limit, the Principal Limit Factor for all HECMs has a floor of 5.0%, regardless of whether the loan has a fixed or adjustable rate. Because of rounding, 5.06% is the lowest rate. Due to rounding and the 5% floor, any Expected Rate of 5.06% or less gives the maximum Principal Limit. 5.06% rounds down to 5.00%, but 5.07% rounds up to 5.125% resulting in less money being available. The HECM has a 120-day rate lock feature such that the swap rate used is the better of the one at application or at closing. The initial credit capacity is much more sensitive to changes in Expected Average Rate than increasing age. For those 90 and above, the same PLF factors are used. (**Chart 14.1**)

FHA Guarantees In the event of lender default, the loan will be assigned to HUD, which will continue to make payments to the borrower based on the original terms of the loan. A HECM is a "non-recourse" loan, which means that a borrower can never owe more than the value of the property at the time the loan is repaid.

FHA Lending Limit In HECM lending, $625,500. Any value in excess is not considered in *Principal Limit* calculations.

Fixed Rate HECM An option selected by homeowner. The note rate will not change during the loan life but the client will not have access to further credit beyond sum drawn at closing. The Expected Rate and Note Rate are identical in fixed rate loans.

HECM Home Equity Conversion Mortgage: FHA-insured reverse mortgage with an open-ended term.

HECM for Purchase An option for purchasing a new principal residence using reverse mortgage financing for a portion of the purchase price.

HELOC Home Equity Line of Credit. This loan requires monthly payments on the interest, or interest and principal and has a closed term.

HECM Line of Credit A revolving line of credit that grows in borrowing power as a dependent variable of the *Ongoing Principal Limit.*

Index An index that is based off the interest rate of a financial instrument or basket of financial instruments. An interest rate index serves as a benchmark used to calculate the interest rate charged on financial products, such as mortgages.

Ineligible Non Borrowing Spouse At application, the mortgagee (Lender) must identify any current Non-Borrowing Spouse and must determine if the Non-Borrowing Spouse is currently eligible or ineligible for a Deferral Period. This determination is a factual determination and cannot be changed or waived by any election. A Non-Borrowing Spouse that meets the FHA qualifying attributes requirements at application for a Deferral Period is an Eligible Non-Borrowing Spouse and may not elect to be ineligible. Similarly, a Non-Borrowing Spouse that is ineligible at application because he or she does not satisfy the requirements for a Deferral Period may not elect to be eligible.

Initial Net Principal Limit Remainder of available credit once set asides(if any) and financed closing costs are deducted from Original Principal Limit.

Initial Principal Limit Funds available at closing based on Age, *Expected Rate*, and *Maximum Claim Amount.*

Initial Rate The beginning index + margin at loan's inception. Also known as the *Note Rate.*

Interest Rate Caps For HECM Annually Adjusting, 5%. For HECM Monthly Adjusting, 10%.

Initial Disbursement Level If homeowner requires more than 60% Year 1, upfront MIP is 2.5% of *Maximum Claim Amount,* if less than 60% Year 1, upfront MIP is 0.5% of Maximum Claim Amount.

Jumbo Reverse Mortgage A proprietary reverse mortgage, not FHA insured, that may be used when FHA guidelines are not suitable, or in which a client's property vastly exceeds the FHA lending limit. These loans usually have higher interest rates, lower loan to value ratios, and restrictions requiring full draws, no line of credit growth, and no revolving access to line of credit once paid down.

Life Estate The right to live in the home, while one or more others own the right to sell the property and to take full possession when the life-estate holder dies or leaves (the "remainder interest"). A HECM can be done on a property where the borrower has only a life estate interest, as long as the owners of the remainder interest agree.

Living Trust A living trust is a legal entity created during a person's lifetime, to hold the ownership of money and real property, often for estate planning purposes. Property held in a living trust may be eligible if the beneficiaries are eligible HECM borrowers.

LESA Life Expectancy Set Asides, either in full or in part, for future tax and insurance payments if client is deemed by underwriter to be deficient in either willingness or capacity to meet homeowner obligations.

Libor The **London Interbank Offered Rate** is the average interest rate estimated by leading banks in London that the average leading bank would be charged if borrowing from other banks. The 1 month Libor commonly is used as an *index* for the monthly Adjustable Rate HECM.

Libor 10 year swap rate Currently used to calculate "Expected Average Rate" in HECM loans.

LTV Ratio of loan amount to home value.

Margin The lender's margin is controlled by the lenders and their investors and may vary from lender to lender and from week to week until loan closing. However, once it is set for a particular loan, it never changes throughout the life of the loan. The margin is constant throughout the life of the mortgage, while the index value is variable. For example, the index might be the 1 month Libor, which varies according to market conditions, and the margin might be 2.25%. If that Libor rate were 1% and the margin 2.25%, the interest rate would be 3.25%.

Maximum Claim Amount Appraised Value of Home, or FHA Lending Limit, whichever is less.

Maximum Fully Indexed Rate For the Adjustable HECM, the Index +Margin+Maximum Periodic Adjustments. The rates will vary throughout the life of the loan but will never exceed the Maximum.

Modified Term Payment Borrower may combine a line of credit with monthly payments for fixed number of months (term option).

Modified Tenure Payment Borrower may combine a line of credit with monthly payments for as long as one borrower remains in the home (tenure option).

Negative Amortization A loan with a growing loan balance. Carrying costs are added to loan balance when no payments are made in any given month. In a HECM this would be draws, interest, monthly MIP, and any fees set aside for servicing or other purposes.

Non Recourse No deficiency judgment may be taken against the borrower or his estate should the loan balance exceed the market value of the property.

Note Rate Index + Margin in Adjustable HECM loans in any given month.

Ongoing Mortgage Insurance Premium (MIP) Calculated on the current loan balance and added on to the loan balance every month.

It is typically an advance from the borrower's available funds. This fee,along with the *Upfront Mortgage Insurance Premium,* provide insurance through FHA to protect both the borrower and lender should the loan balance exceed the home value. Today the rate is 1.25%. The money becomes part of FHA's mortgage insurance fund. This fund is used to pay claims to lenders if the borrower's loan balance exceeds their home value at the time the loan is paid off. When the loan balance reaches 98% of the Maximum Claim Amount, the lender may assign the loan to HUD and be paid the full loan balance from the mortgage insurance fund. This protection makes the HECM possible for lenders, who now have minimal risk of loss, regardless of what happens to the borrower's home value.

Ongoing Principal Limit Growing credit capacity during HECM loan life tied to *EFFECTIVE RATE.*

Origination Fee The origination fee compensates the lender for the activities involved in setting up the loan.

Although origination fees in the forward mortgage world are typically 1% or less, the origination fee for HECMs is permitted by FHA to be as much as: **2% of the first 200,000 of Maximum Claim Amount plus 1% of additional home value BUT not more than $6000 total.** Lenders may always charge **at least $2,500** on lower value homes and lenders may offer to waive or reduce origination fees. *This fee can be negotiated.*

Principal Limit Factor Table of values used by FHA to determine how much the *Initial Principal Limit* will be based on Age and *Expected Rate.* Applied to *Maximum Claim Amount.*

Appendix Table 1 - Principal Limits Given Lookup Rates
Assuming a $300,000 home with a 2.25% margin

10-Year Swap Rate	Lookup Rate	Age 63	Age 68	Age 73	Age 78	Age 83	Age 88
2.81%	5.000%	$159,300	$166,200	$173,700	$180,000	$187,500	$195,000
2.94%	5.125%	$153,900	$161,100	$169,500	$176,400	$184,200	$192,300
3.06%	5.250%	$149,400	$157,200	$165,300	$172,800	$181,200	$189,300
3.19%	5.375%	$144,900	$153,300	$162,000	$169,500	$178,200	$186,900
3.31%	5.500%	$141,600	$150,000	$158,700	$166,200	$175,500	$184,500
3.44%	5.625%	$138,000	$146,700	$156,000	$163,200	$172,500	$182,700
3.56%	5.750%	$134,100	$142,800	$152,100	$160,800	$170,100	$180,600
3.69%	5.875%	$130,800	$140,100	$149,100	$158,100	$167,700	$178,200
3.81%	6.000%	$127,500	$136,800	$147,000	$155,400	$165,300	$176,400
3.94%	6.125%	$124,800	$133,800	$143,700	$152,700	$163,200	$174,300
4.06%	6.250%	$121,500	$130,800	$141,000	$150,300	$161,100	$172,500

Chart courtesy of Gerald Wagner, PhD, President of IBIS Software.

Repair Set-Asides: If property does not meet Minimum Property Standards, the borrower must complete required repairs. If the cost of the repairs is **less than 15% of the Maximum Claim Amount**, the borrower may complete the work **after closing**. In these cases, the lender attaches a "repair rider" to the Loan Agreement, certifying that the work will be completed as required. A **repair set-aside** of **150% of the estimated cost of the repairs** is established, and this credit is not available for any other purpose until the repairs are complete and approved. Once repairs have been inspected, and contractors paid, any remaining amount will convert to available credit.

Seasoning: Lenders may only permit the payoff of existing non-HECM liens using HECM proceeds if the liens have been in place longer for 12 months or resulted in less than $500 cash to the mortgagor, whether at closing or through cumulative draws (e.g., as with a Home Equity Line of Credit (HELOC)) prior to the date of the initial HECM loan application.

Set-Asides: Set-asides are **not costs**, because they do not immediately become part of the loan balance. Instead, they represent **money reserved for a future purpose**. The amounts will be added to the loan balance only when the funds are drawn.

Service Fee Set-Aside (SFSA): If a servicing fee is charged, the lender sets aside from the borrower's principal limit the present value of the total monthly servicing fees from closing until the borrower would reach age 100, taking into account the growth of the principal limit. **This reduces the funds available to the borrower at closing**, typically by $4000-6000. This amount is not debt, so it is NOT added to the loan balance at closing. Instead, it is set aside or held in reserve so that it cannot be spent in other ways. The loan servicer deducts its monthly fee from this credit amount and adds it to the loan balance each month during the life of the loan. Few borrowers live to age 100, therefore, the total amount set aside by the HECM program typically inflates the actual total amount likely to be charged on most HECMs during the life of the loan. If the loan is paid off early, the remaining amount in the

SFSA is like the line of credit ; it reverts to equity. In other words, the set-aside is money that has not been borrowed.. There is no refund of the SFSA because it was never charged to the borrower in the first place. Most new HECM loans do not require a service fee set-aside.

Servicer The entity that administers the loan after closing, maintaining records and issuing statements.

TALC Total Annual Loan Cost . The TALC rate is an annual percentage cost of a reverse mortgage. Different than (APR),which takes into account only the finance charges in a credit transaction, the TALC rate considers all costs. In projecting the total cost of credit, TALC rates are based on different loan periods such as two years, a period equal to the youngest consumer's life expectancy, and a period equal to 1.4 times the youngest consumer's life expectancy. TALC rates are based on assumed annual house appreciation rates of 0 percent, 4 percent, and 8 percent. The projected total cost of credit must reflect all costs and charges to the consumer, including the costs of any annuity that the consumer purchases as part of the reverse mortgage transaction. In general, the longer the borrower remains in the house, the lower the total annual loan cost will be.

Term Payment Borrower receives monthly payments from the lender for a period of months selected by the borrower. If the lender is late making the payment, the borrower is owed a late fee.

Tenure Payment Borrower receives monthly payments from the lender for as long as the home is occupied as the principal residence. Although the loan balance is scheduled to equal the principal limit when the youngest borrower reaches age 100, payments continue for as long as the borrower lives in the home as a principal residence, no matter how long that is. In effect, the homeowner has used his home, rather than his cash, to create an annuity, but an annuity that is not portable to a new residence. If the lender is late sending the payment, the borrower is owed a late fee.

Time Value of Money. The concept that the value of a dollar to be received in future is less than the value of a dollar on hand today. One reason is that money received today can be **invested** thus generating more money.

Upfront Mortgage Insurance Premium (MIP) Calculated on *Maximum Claim Amount* and added to loan balance, unless paid outside of closing. Depending on how much of the *Initial Principal Limit* is drawn, the UFMIP will be either .5% or 2.5%. This fee, along with the *Ongoing Mortgage Insurance Premium,* provide insurance through FHA to protect both the borrower and lender should the loan balance exceed the home value.

Appendix for Advanced Study

Courtesy of www.toolsforretirementplanning.com

Research from Gerald Wagner and Barry and Stephen Sacks

A variety of strategies can be used to fund spending when combining reverse mortgages and portfolio draws. Wagner's paper examines 5 strategies, such as a using the reverse mortgage line of credit first before any portfolio withdrawals, fixed monthly draws for 30 years, or monthly tenure advance guaranteed to continue as long as the homeowner stays in the house. All the strategies improved retirement withdrawals. Benefits of each strategy are examined.

Wagner, Gerald C. 2013. "The 6.0 % Rule." Journal of Financial Planning, 26(12): 46 – 54.

With only the portfolio to fund spending, sustainable withdrawals were 3.75%. In contrast, "With a 30-year spending horizon and first-year withdrawal of 6.0 %, reverse mortgage scheduled advances as a portfolio supplement give "spending success" levels of 88 to 92 %. Even with a first-year withdrawal of 6.5 %, success levels are still 83 to 86 %. This paper provides financial planners with a review of the relative merits of using a reverse mortgage as a retirement spending supplement. After 15 years, the client's estate value is 10 to 30% higher using the reverse mortgage plus portfolio than relying on the portfolio alone, combining current portfolio, home value and deducting the reverse mortgage loan balance.

http://www.onefpa.org/journal/Pages/December-2013-The-6-0-%-Rule.aspx

Sacks, Barry H., and Stephen R. Sacks. 2012. "Reversing the Conventional Wisdom: Using Home Equity to Supplement Retirement Income." Journal of Financial Planning 25(2): 43-52.

"This paper examines three strategies for using home equity, in the form of a reverse mortgage credit line, to increase the safe maximum initial rate of retirement income withdrawals." http://www.onefpa.org/journal/Pages/Reversing%20the%20Conventional%20Wisdom%20Using%20Home%20Equity%20to%20Supplement%20Retirement%20Income.aspx

Standby Reverse Mortgage: Borrow from then repay Line of Credit to augment Portfolio withdrawals.

A Standby Reverse Mortgage is a strategy of borrowing from the HECM Line of Credit when the portfolio has suffered a significant downturn and repaying it after the portfolio recovers so it is available to help future spending in the future. The team of Salter, Pfeiffer and Evensky introduced this concept.

Pfeiffer, Shaun, C. Angus Schaal, and John Salter. 2014. "HECM Reverse Mortgages: Now or Last Resort?" Journal of Financial Planning 27(5) 44-51.

"This study outlines recent changes in the reverse mortgage market and investigates plan survival rates for distribution strategies that establish a Home Equity Conversion Mortgage (HECM) reverse mortgage line of credit at the beginning of retirement and as a last resort. Early establishment of an HECM line of credit in the current low interest rate environment is shown to consistently provide higher 30-year survival rates than those shown for the last resort strategies. The early establishment survival advantage for real withdrawal rates at or above 5 % is estimated to begin between 15 and 20 years after loan origination and is shown to be as high as 31 %age points, or 85 %, greater than the last resort survival rates."

Pfeiffer, Shaun, John Salter, and Harold Evensky. 2013 "Increasing the Sustainable Withdrawal Rate Using the Standby Reverse Mortgage." Journal of Financial Planning 26(12): 55-62.

"Sustainable withdrawal rates jumped from 3.15% to 5 and 6% with a standby HECM Line of Credit. The real key, not directly addressed in the article, is the size of the line of credit in realation to the portfolio. Clients had an important boost in sustainable spending with a line of credit as small as 8% – 10% of the portfolio. The authors note "The findings from this research suggest that the adage of using a reverse mortgage as a last resort could be a huge mistake in a rising interest rate environment where a retiree waits to set up a line of credit in the future."

http://www.onefpa.org/journal/Pages/December-2013-Increasing-the-Sustainable-Withdrawal-Rate-Using-the-Standby-Reverse-Mortgage.aspx

Research from Wade Pfau, PhD, on HECM Line of Credit

https://tcbdavison.files.wordpress.com/2015/02/hidden_value_of_reverse_mortgage_standby_line_of_credit.pdf